CHAMPAK
little fingers
Big Brains
Kindergarten

 ★ My name is

MOONSTONE

Published in Moonstone
by Rupa Publications India Pvt. Ltd 2023
7/16, Ansari Road, Daryaganj
New Delhi 110002

Sales centres:
Bengaluru Chennai
Hyderabad Jaipur Kathmandu
Kolkata Mumbai Prayagraj

P-ISBN: 978-93-5702-280-4
E-ISBN: 978-93-5702-274-3

Second impression 2025

10 9 8 7 6 5 4 3 2

Printed in India

Skills Covered

Cognitive Development

- ⭐ Maze
- ⭐ Sequencing
- ⭐ Odd one out
- ⭐ Direction
- ⭐ Do as directed
- ⭐ Colour code
- ⭐ What goes together
- ⭐ Spot the difference
- ⭐ Find the hidden pictures
- ⭐ Patterns
- ⭐ Coding

- ⭐ Cognitive development refers to a child's capacity to engage in critical thinking, comprehend, express, recollect, visualise, and anticipate future outcomes.
- ⭐ Cognitive development fosters problem-solving, critical thinking, hand-eye coordination, and spatial awareness.
- ⭐ Worksheets that focus on sequence, pattern, direction, and spotting differences offer logical thinking, decision-making, and task persistence.
- ⭐ These skills aid children in their ability to apply and evaluate information.
- ⭐ They empower a child to follow instructions, experiment, unleash their creativity, and cultivate a habit of continuous learning and growth.

Pre-Writing

- ⭐ Standing line
- ⭐ Sleeping line
- ⭐ Slanting line
- ⭐ Humps
- ⭐ Curves
- ⭐ Zig zag
- ⭐ Mountain pattern

- ⭐ Pre-writing skills are fundamental for a child to develop before they begin to write.
- ⭐ These skills contribute to the child's ability to hold and use a pencil, and the ability to draw, write, copy, and colour.
- ⭐ A major component of pre-writing shapes arve:
  I, —, ~~~~, /, \, /\/\/\, \/\/\/,))), ⌢⌢

Numeracy

- ⭐ Numbers 1-30
- ⭐ Missing numbers
- ⭐ More or less
- ⭐ Count and write
- ⭐ Up and down
- ⭐ After numbers

- ⭐ Identify, recognise, and count numbers 1-30.
- ⭐ Assign values to numbers up to 20. Identify and recognise number names.
- ⭐ Facilitates the growth of skills related to comparing quantities.
- ⭐ Young learners can grasp the fundamentals of up and down, tall and short through relatable tasks.

Skills Covered

EVS

- ⭐ Animals
- ⭐ Aquatic animals
- ⭐ Community helpers
- ⭐ Transport
- ⭐ Seasons
- ⭐ Vegetables
- ⭐ Fruits

- ⭐ The worksheets help children recognise, name and differentiate between common fruits and vegetables.
- ⭐ Recognise and identify pets, farms, aquatic and wild animals, their habitat, and their young ones.
- ⭐ Name and identify different community helpers with the tools they use.
- ⭐ Identify and name different modes of transport.
- ⭐ Identify and name the four seasons, along with the clothes and the activities that form a part of each season.

Pre- Math

- ⭐ Shapes
- ⭐ Colour
- ⭐ In and out
- ⭐ Big and small
- ⭐ Same and different

- ⭐ Pre-math activity sheets help them apply mathematical concepts to daily life scenarios.
- ⭐ It allows a child to sort out shapes by their attributes.
- ⭐ It helps distinguish objects by shapes, size, pattern, and colour.
- ⭐ It helps develop visual differences, following directions, and problem-solving skills.

Literacy

- ⭐ Letters Aa - Zz
- ⭐ Beginning sound
- ⭐ Missing letters

- ⭐ Alphabetic awareness helps a child identify letters and their formation , the beginning sound of each letter, and the objects related to them.
- ⭐ Associating letters with sounds creates a foundation for reading.
- ⭐ Missing letters help a child memorise the sequence of letters Aa-Zz.

⭐ Who am I?

My name is _____

I am a  □ □

I am _____ years old.

My birthday is on _____

My favourite colour is

(colour the circle)

Pre-Writing

Follow the standing lines to guide the butterflies to the flowers

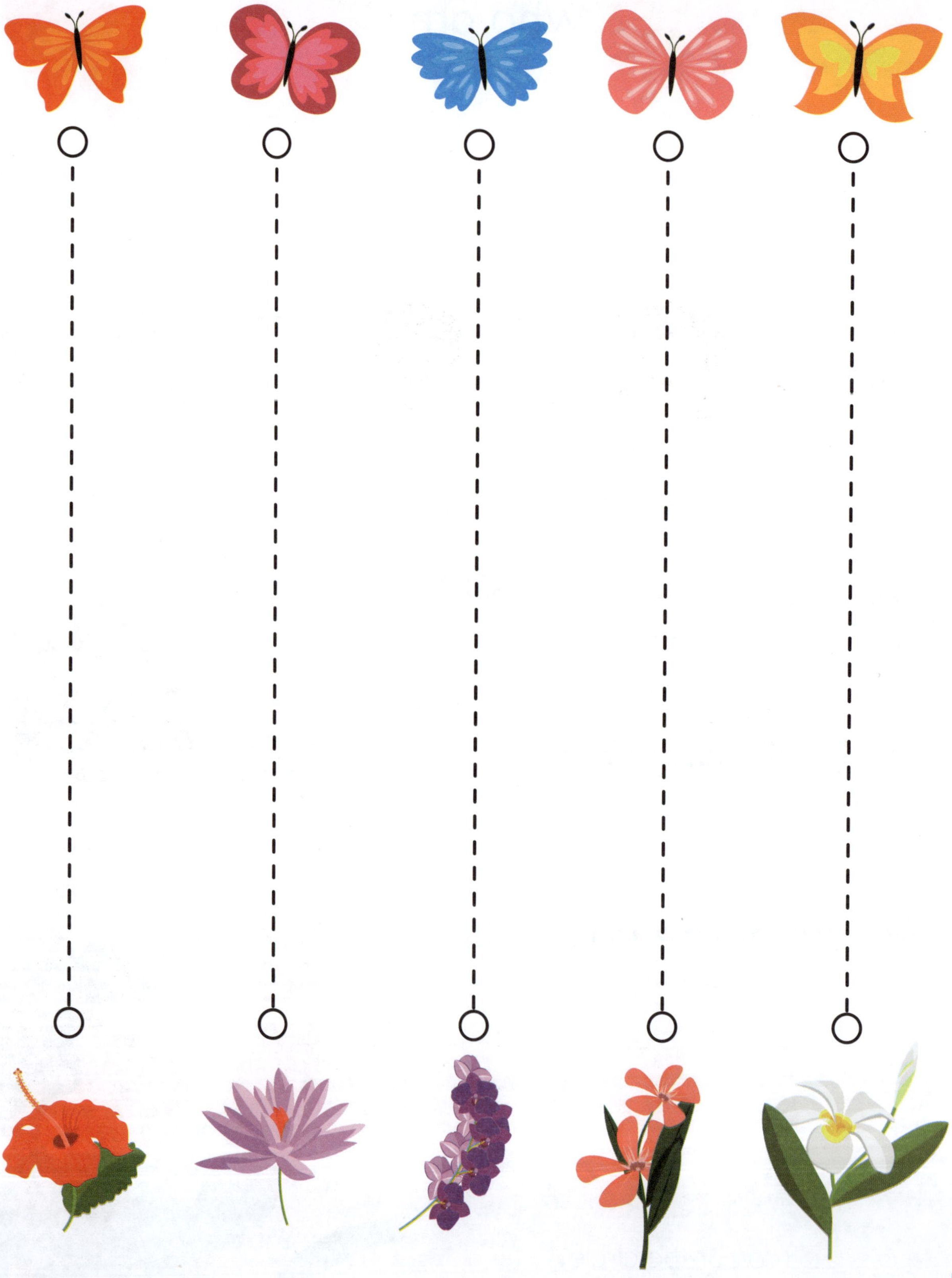

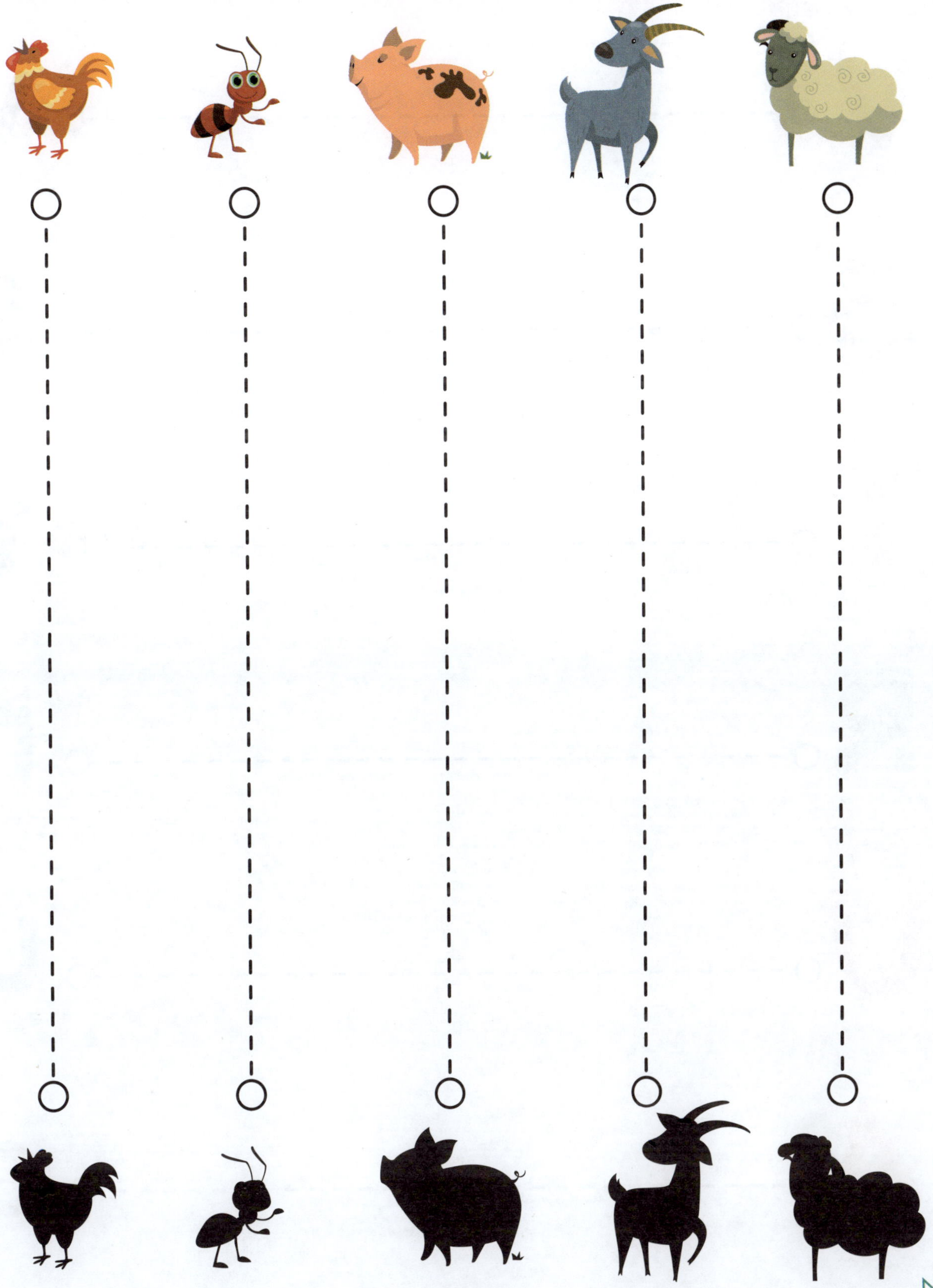

V o- - - - - - - - - - - - - - - - - -o v

S o- - - - - - - - - - - - - - - - - -o s

T o- - - - - - - - - - - - - - - - - -o t

R o- - - - - - - - - - - - - - - - - -o r

U o- - - - - - - - - - - - - - - - - -o u

A o- - - - - - - - - - - - - - - - - -o a

4

Pre-Writing

Take the animals to their food by tracing the slanting lines

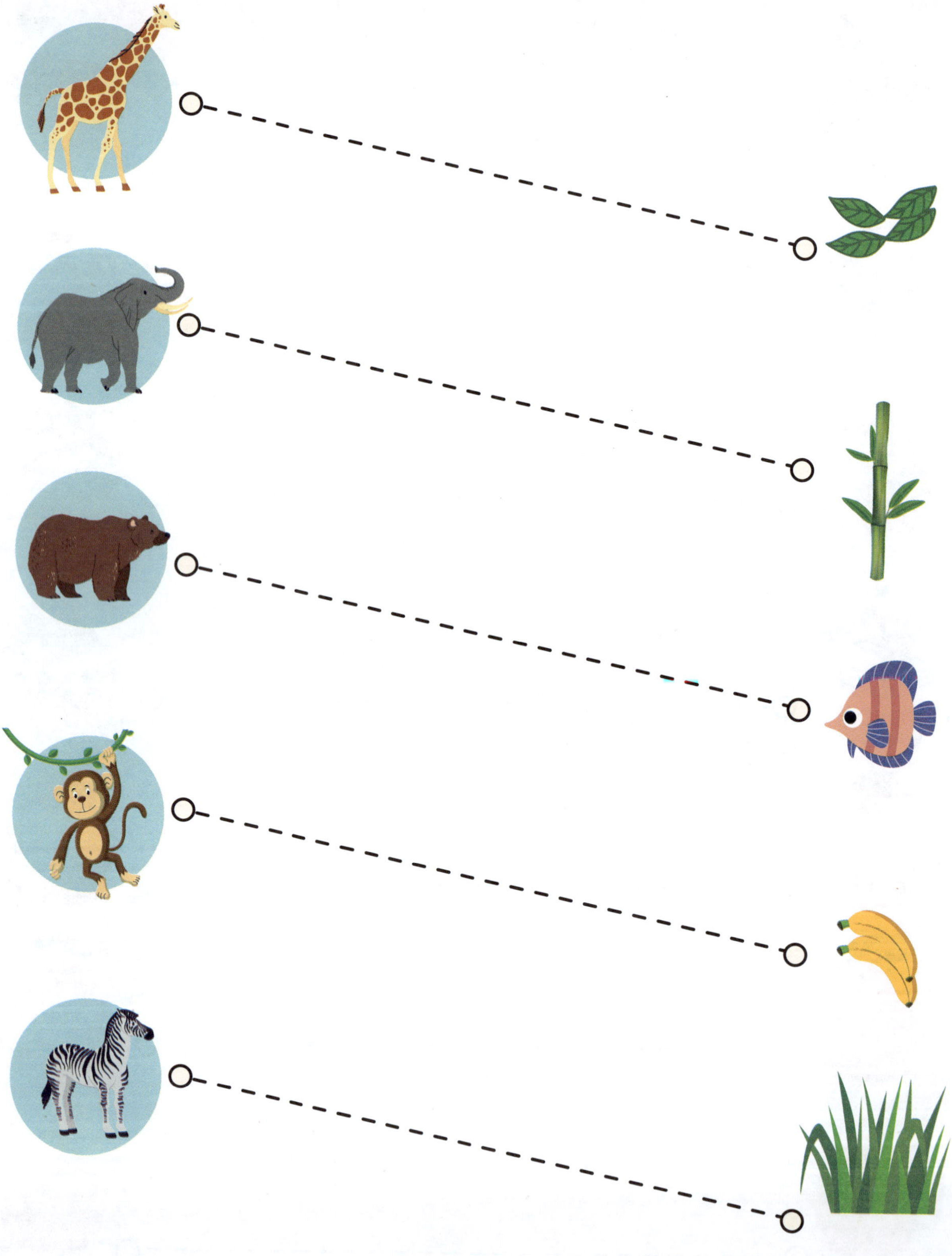

Match the things that go together by tracing the slanting lines

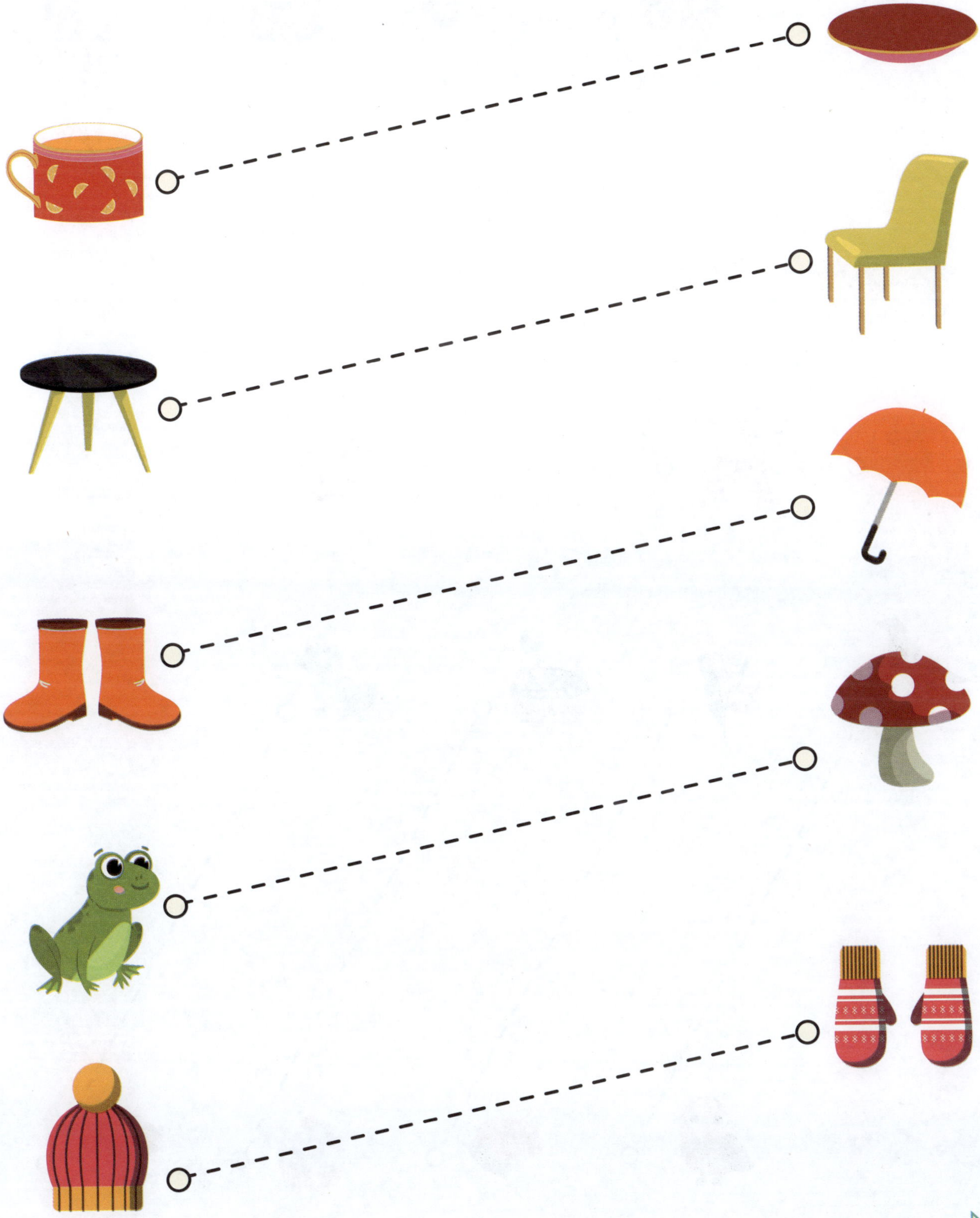

Pre-Writing

Trace the slanting lines

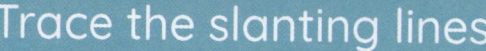

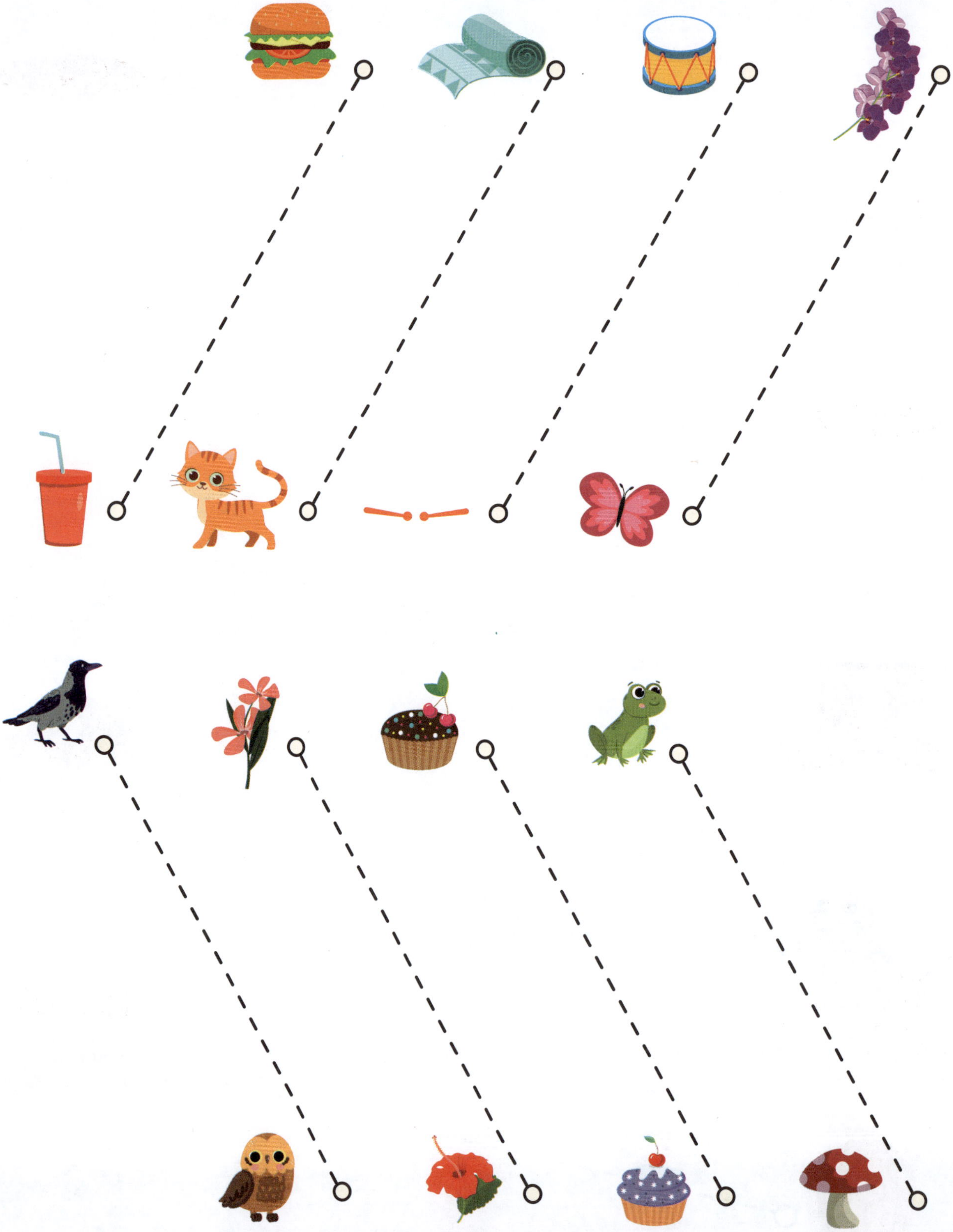

Trace the pattern

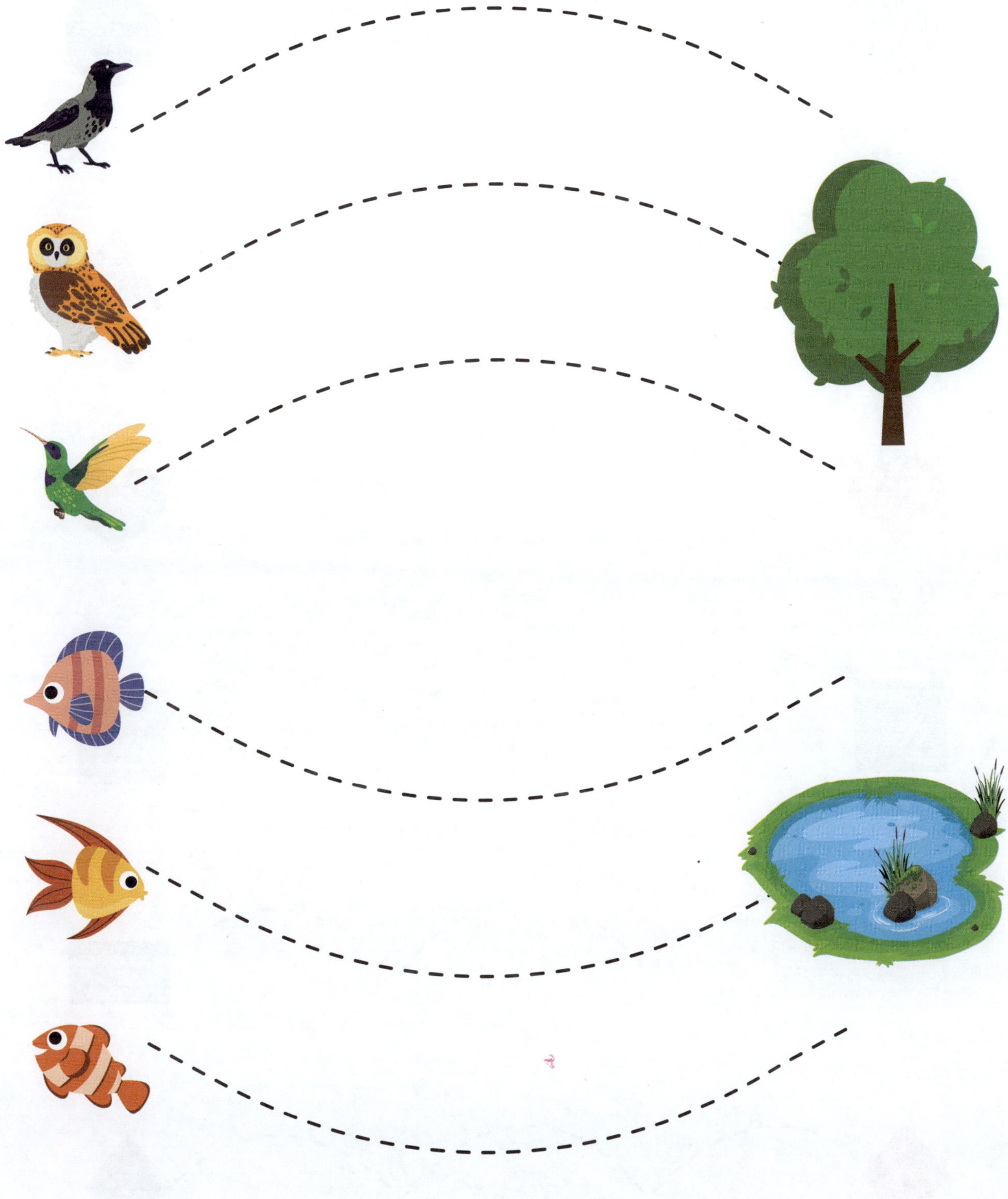

Trace the humps

10

Help our pig find the sty

Trace the patterns

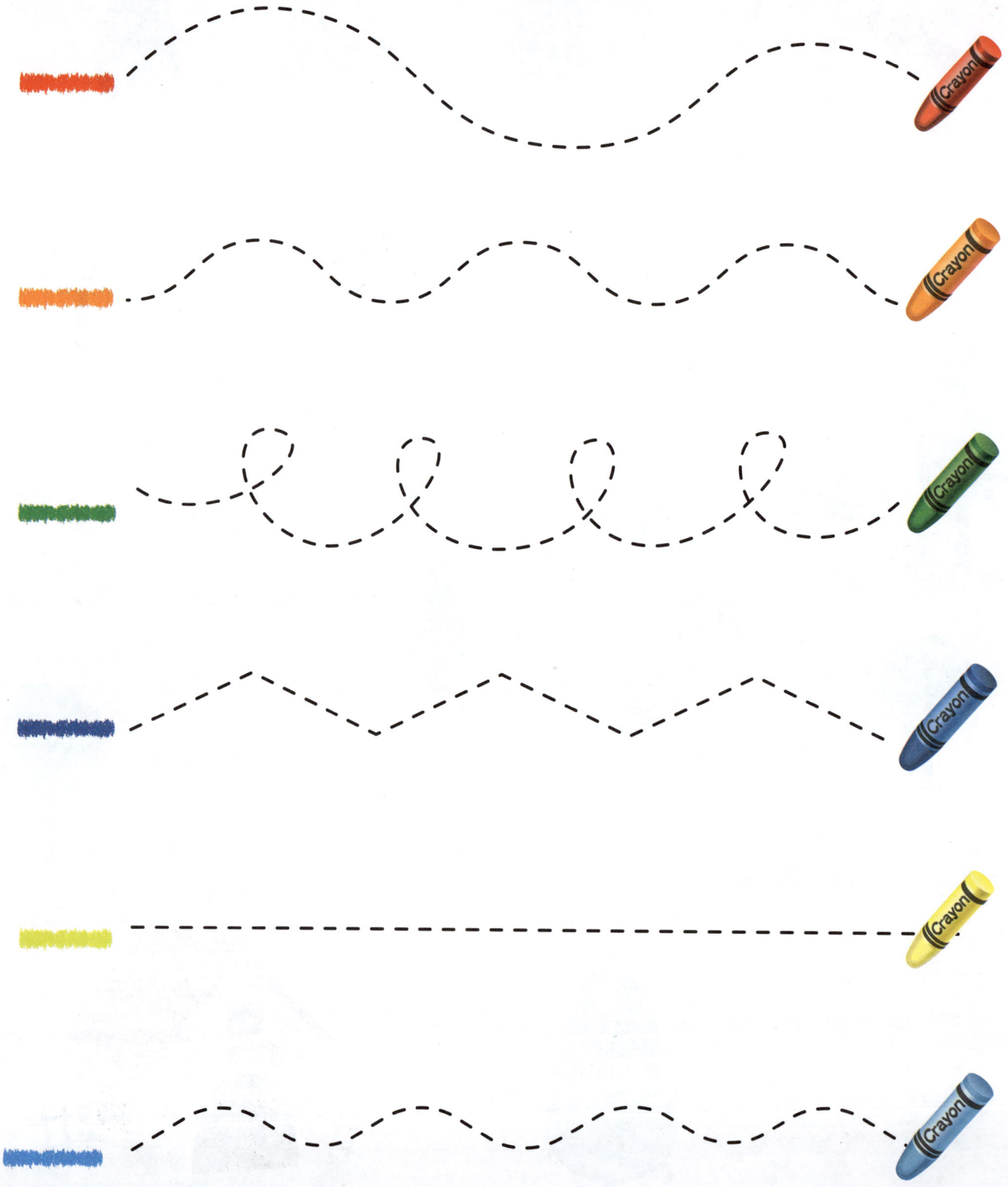

Literacy

Trace the letters A-Z

A B C D

E F G H

I J K L

M N O P

Q R S T

U V W X

Y Z

Cognitive Development

Number the pictures sequence-wise

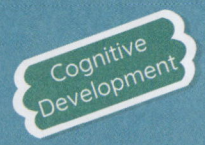

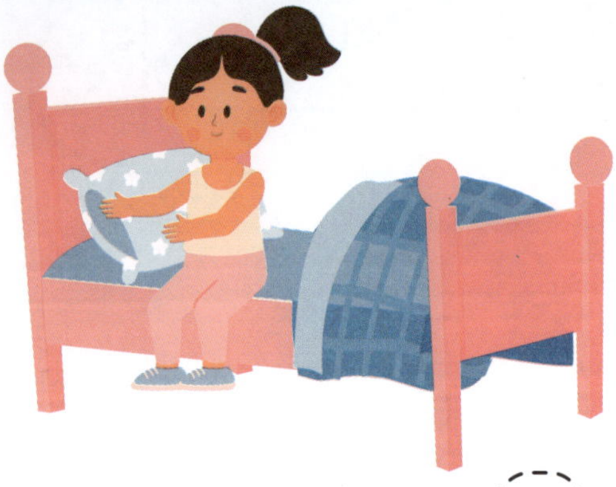

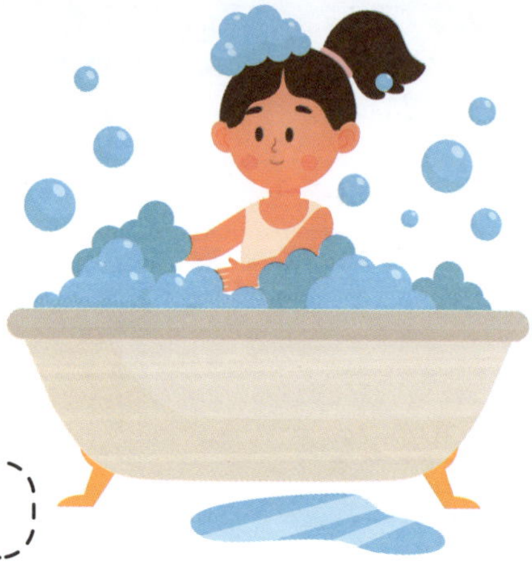

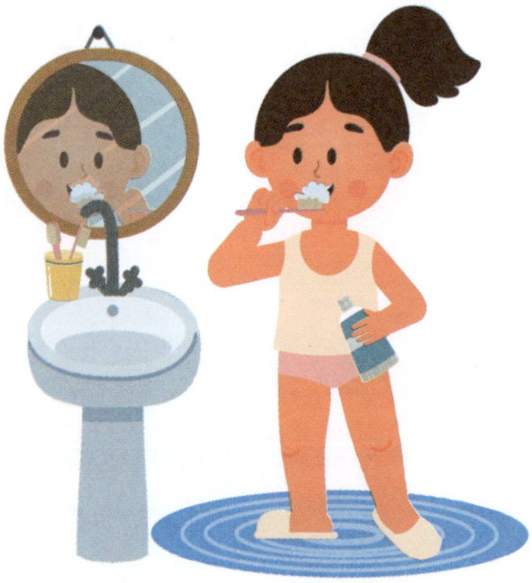

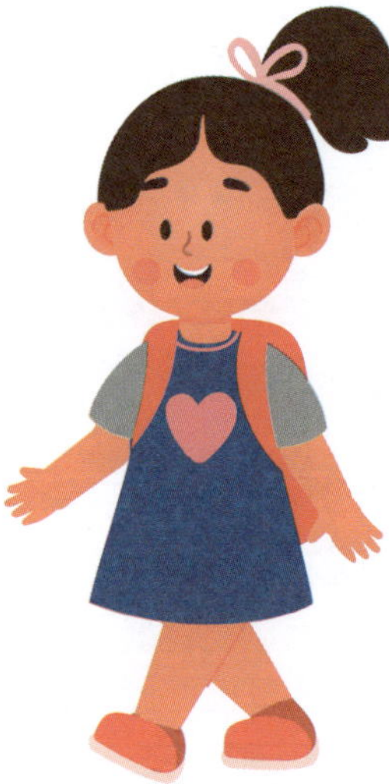

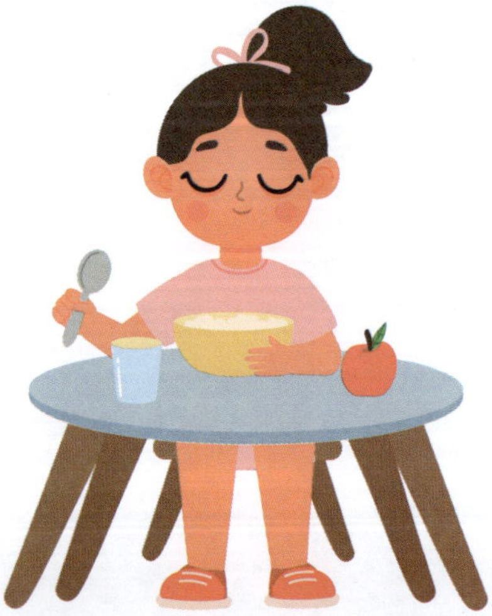

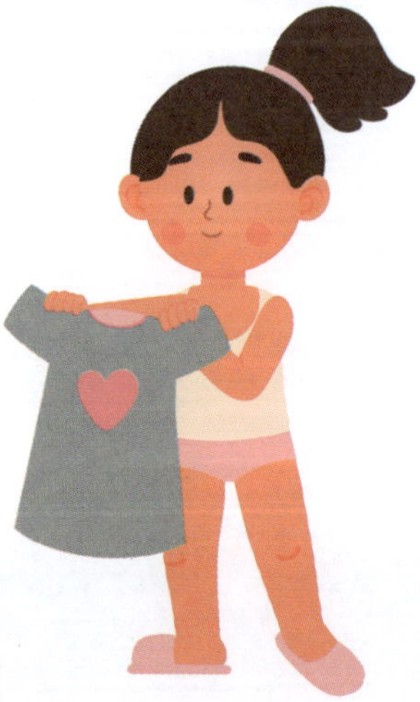

Circle the odd one out

Circle all the circles in the picture

1	11	21	31	41
2	12	22	32	42
3	13	23	33	43
4	14	24	34	44
5	15	25	35	45
6	16	26	36	46
7	17	27	37	47
8	18	28	38	48
9	19	29	39	49
10	20	30	40	50

Match the animals with their young ones

Giraffe

Monkey

lion

Elephant

Bear

Calf

Cub

Cub

Infant

Calf

18

Cognitive Development

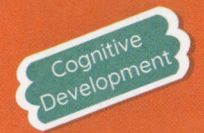

Colour the shapes according to the colour codes given below

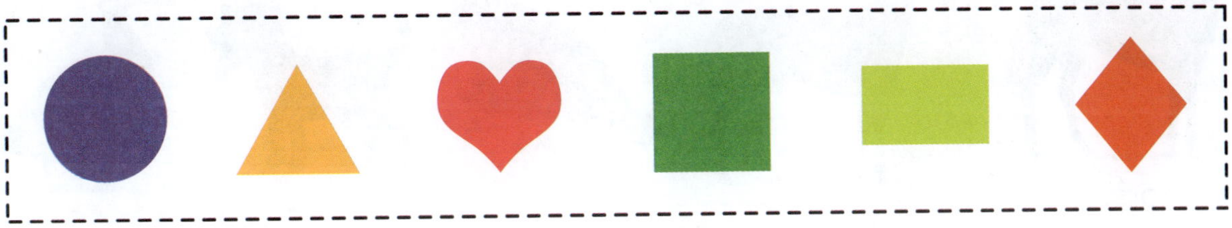

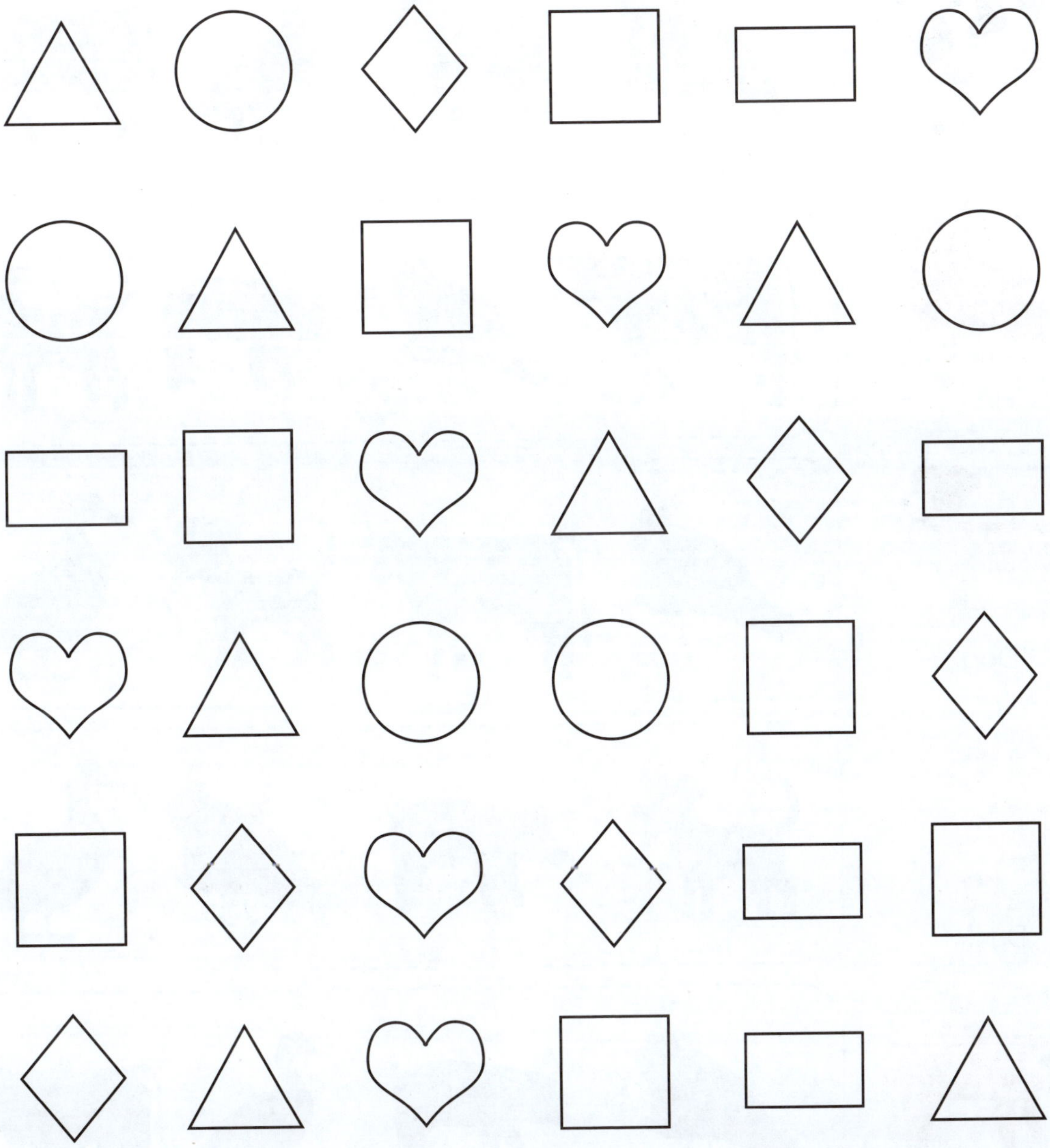

EVS

Circle the correct shadow

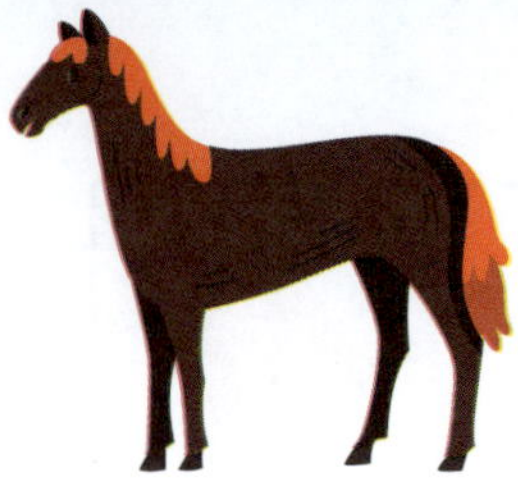

Horse

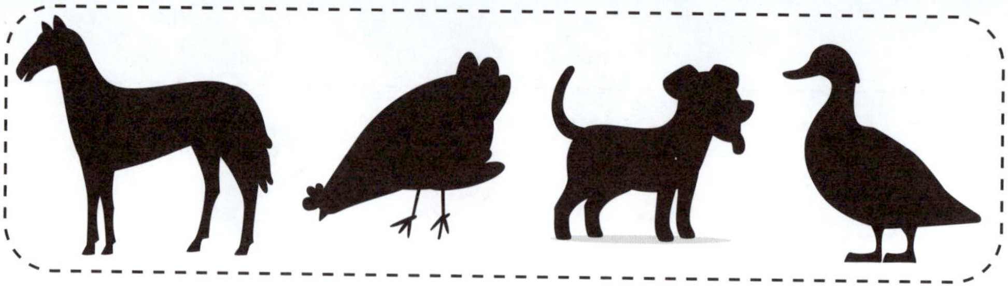

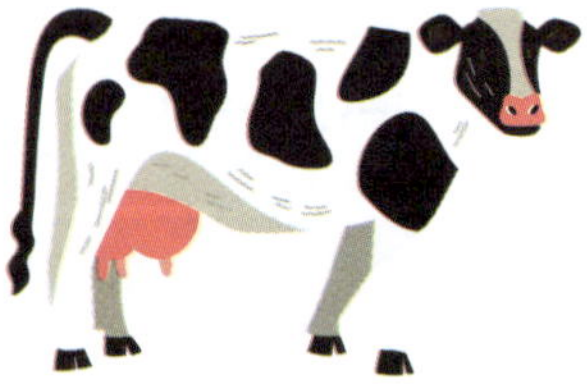

Cow

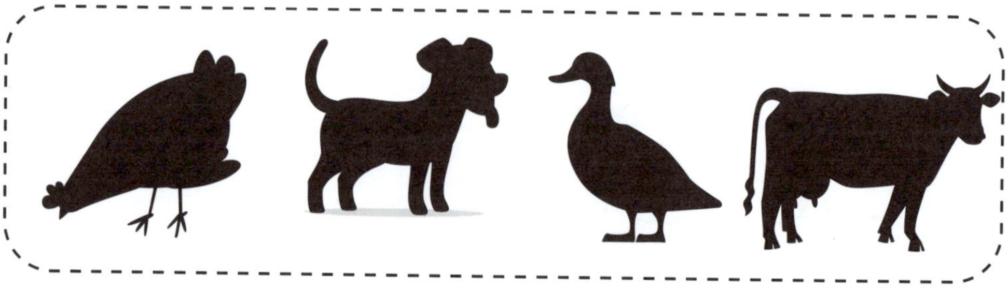

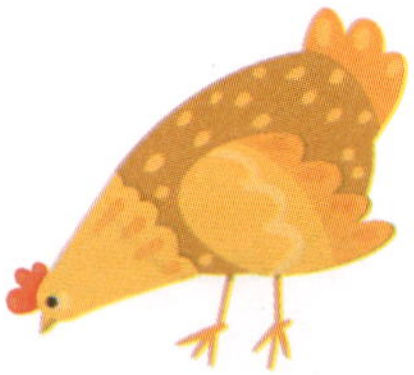

Hen

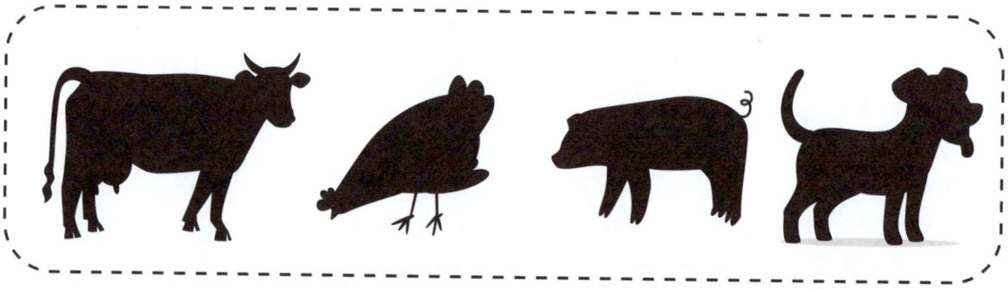

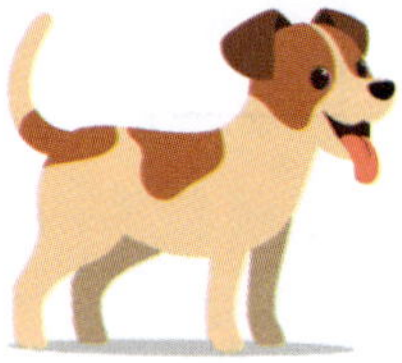

Dog

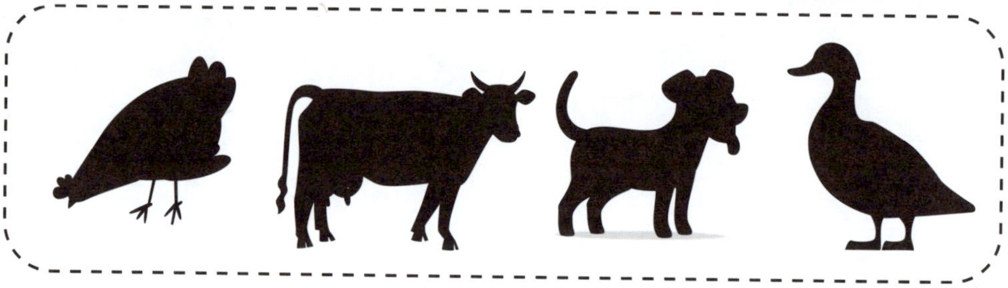

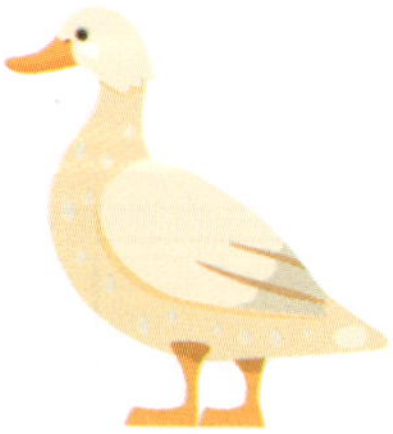

Duck

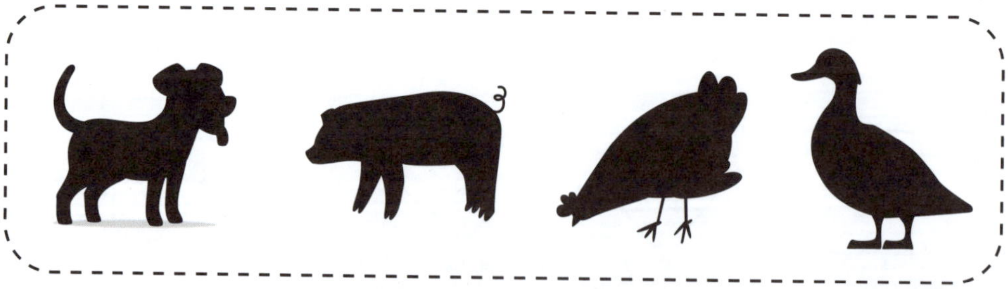

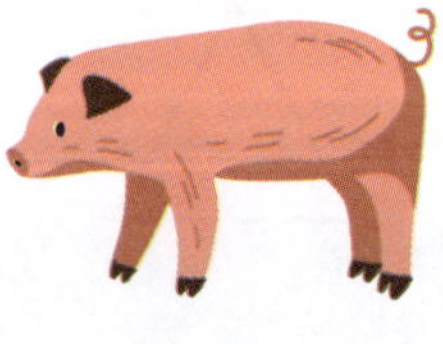

Pig

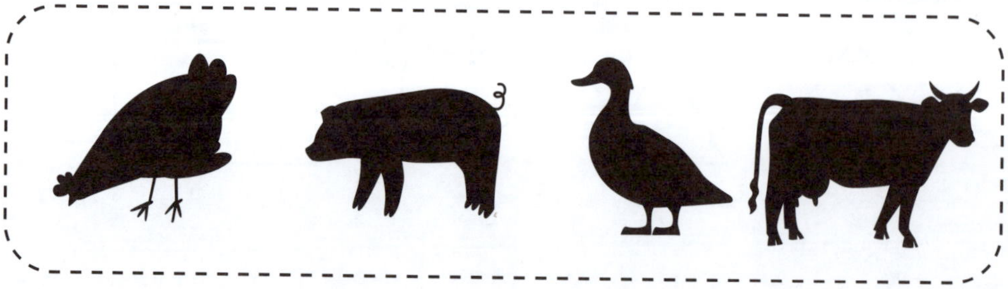

Colour the arrows facing right in blue and the arrows facing left in red

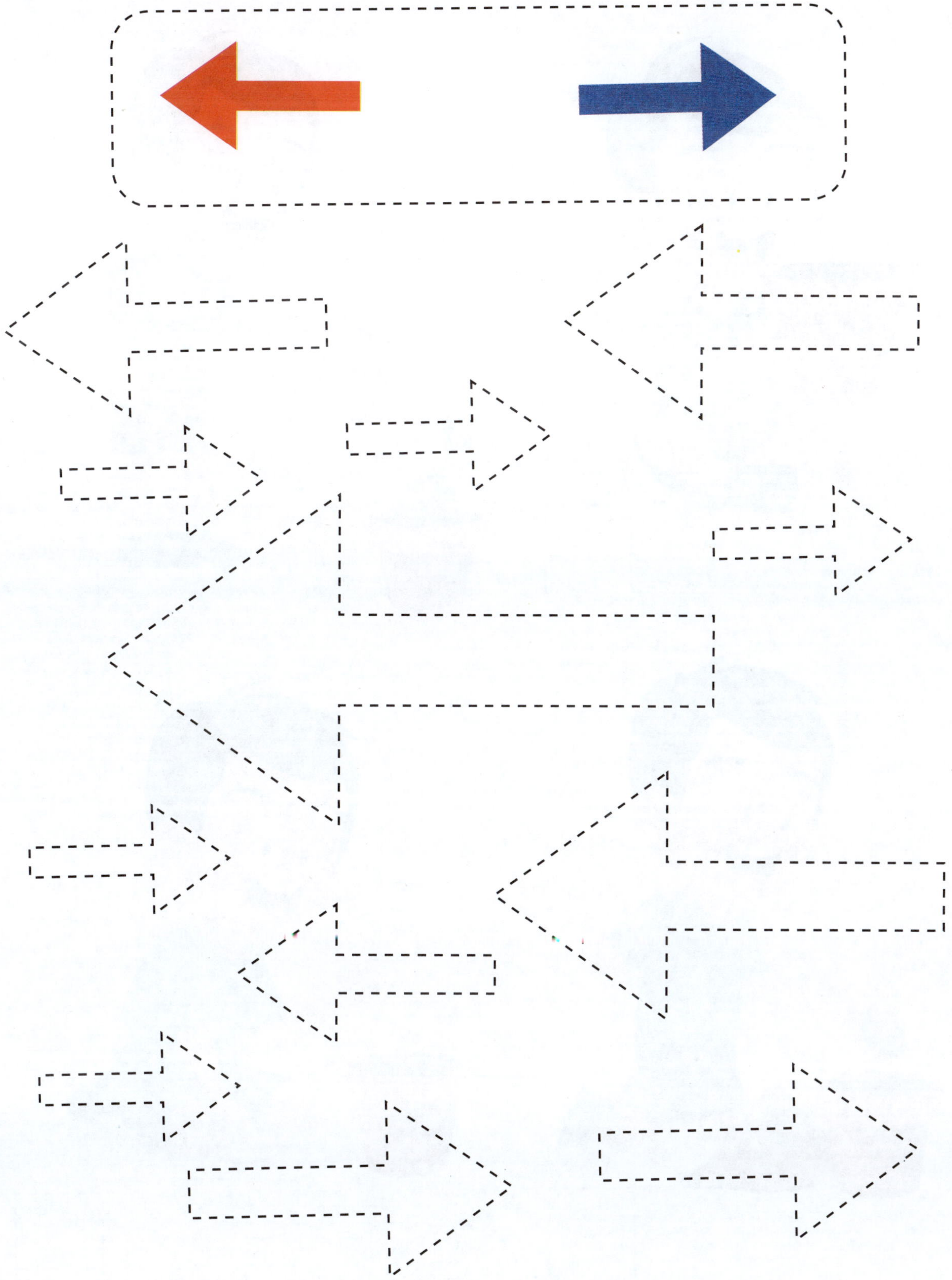

Cognitive Development

Number the pictures in the correct order

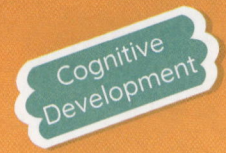

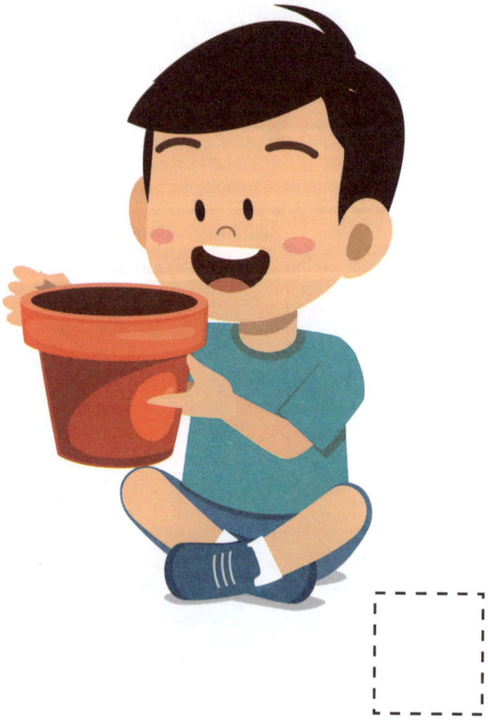

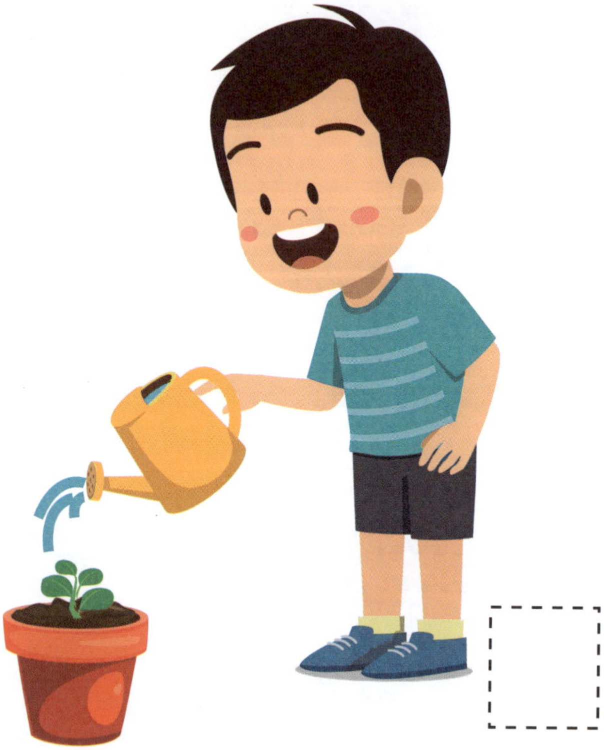

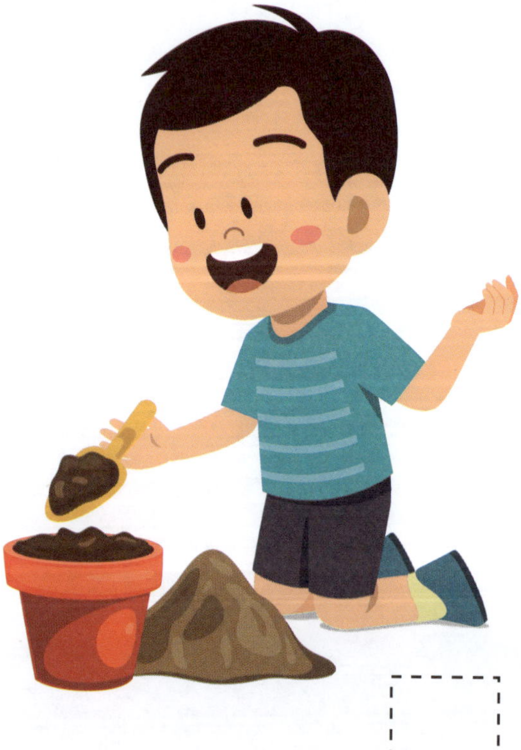

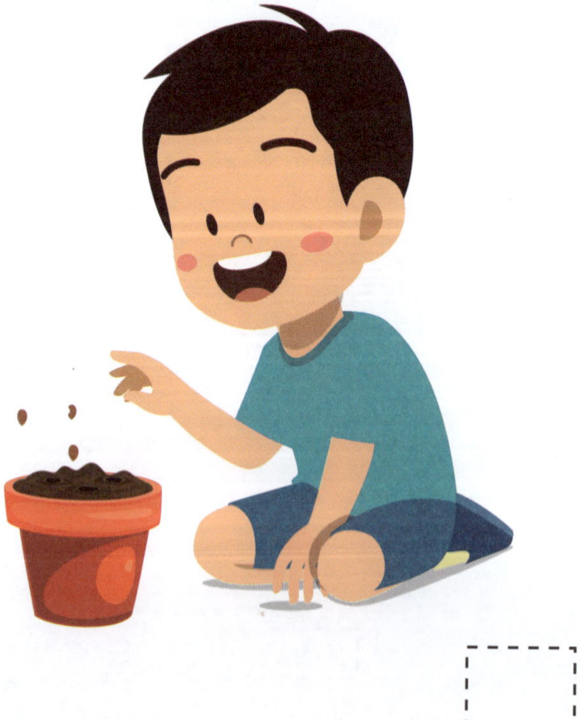

EVS

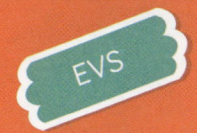

Match each community helper with their tools

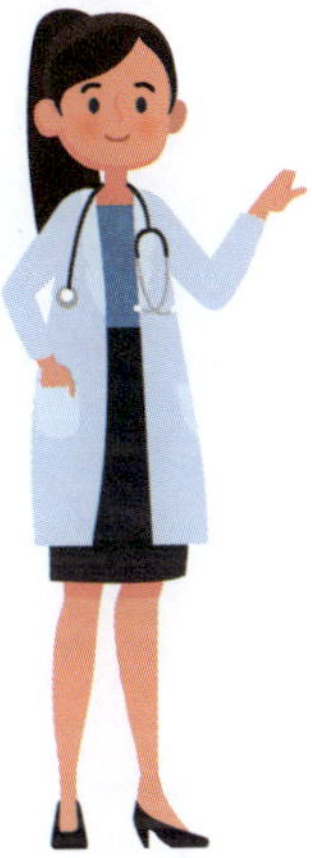

Doctor

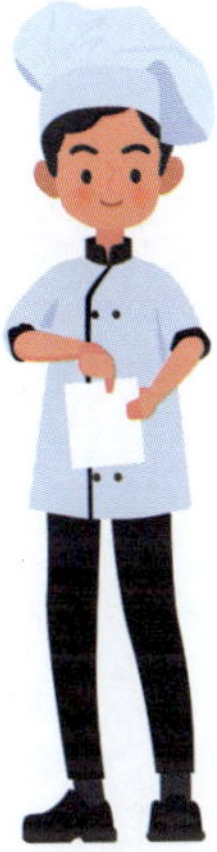

Chef

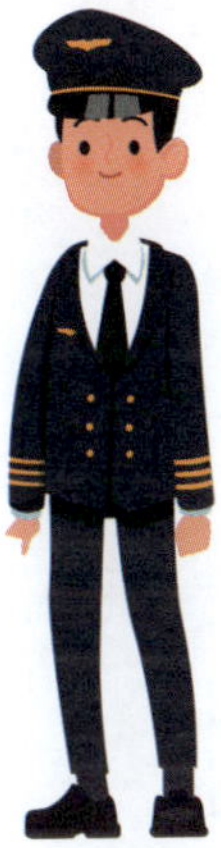

Pilot

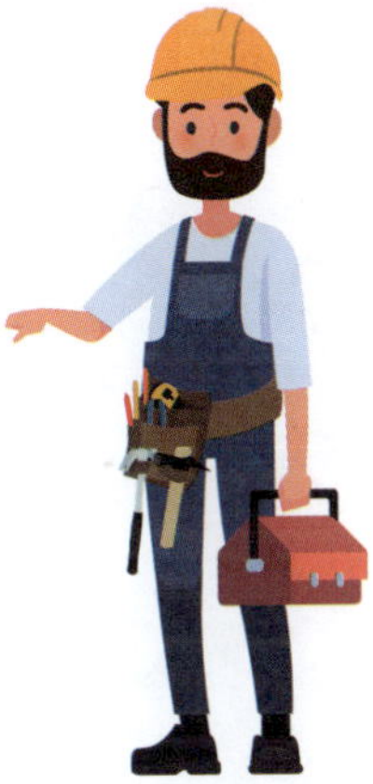

Carpenter

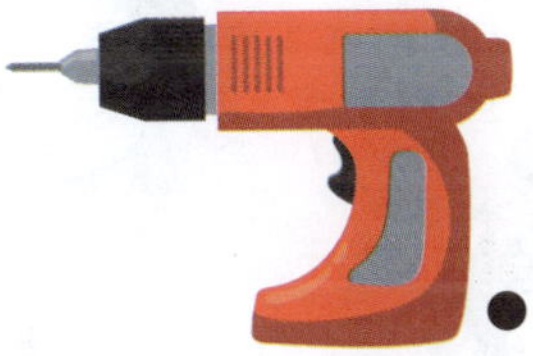

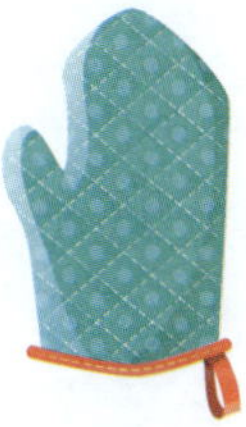

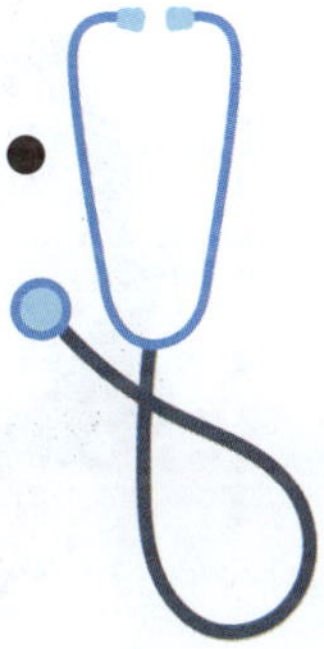

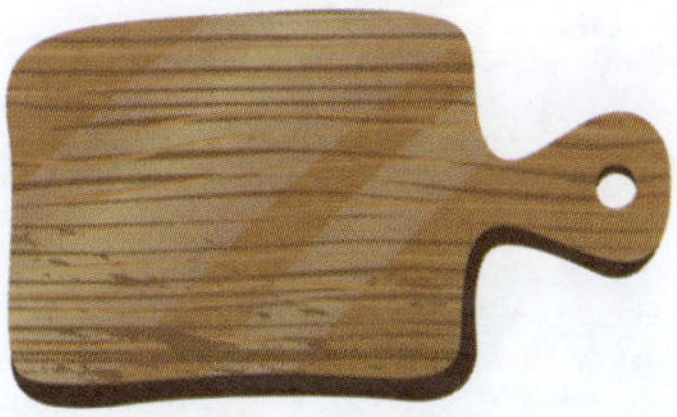

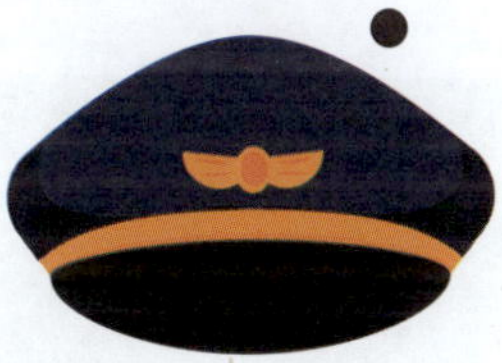

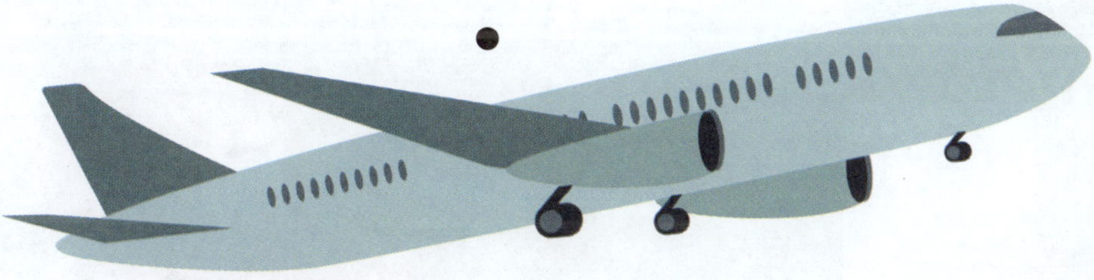

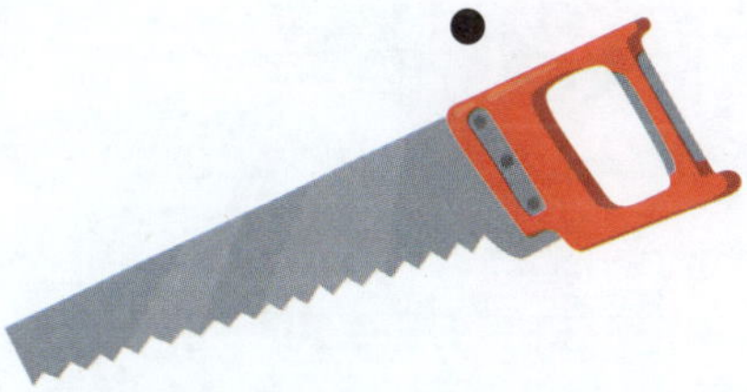

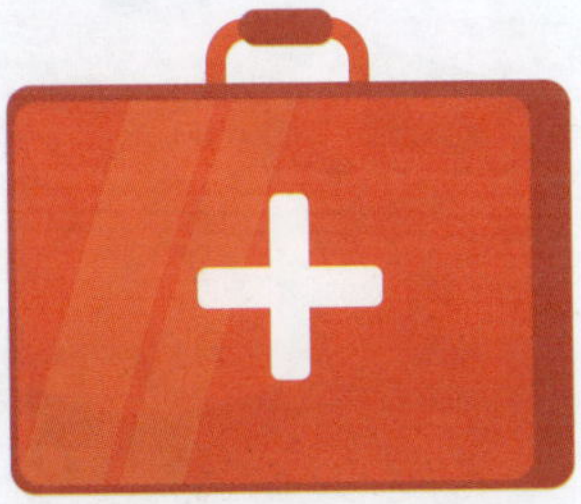

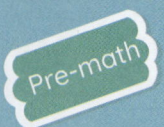

Trace the shapes and colour them

EVS

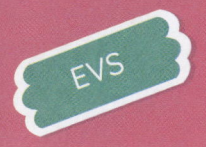

Identify and match the footprints

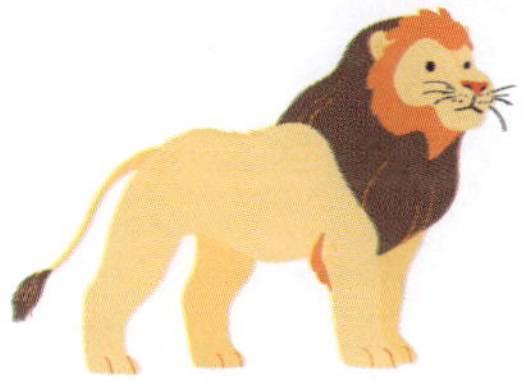

Lion

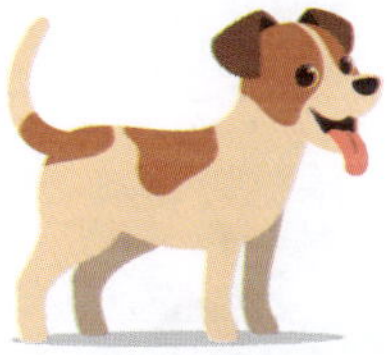

Dog

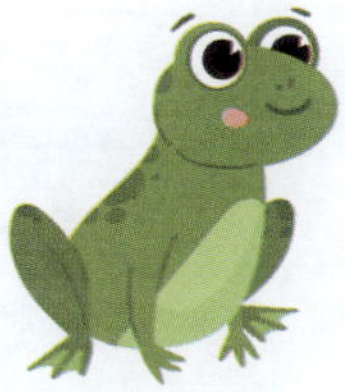

Frog

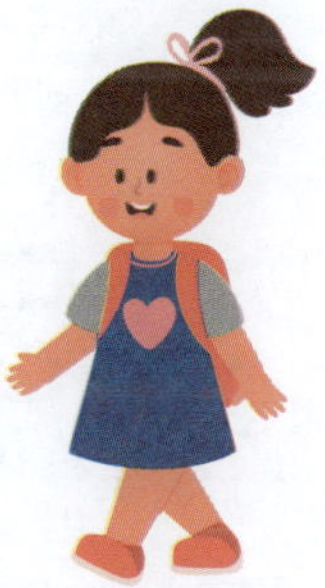

Human

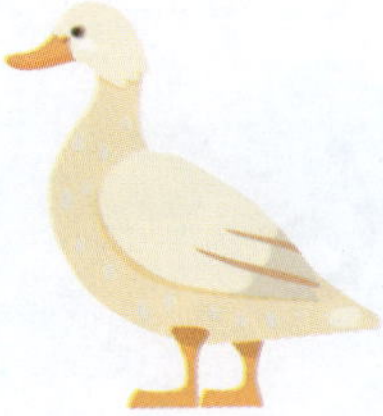

Duck

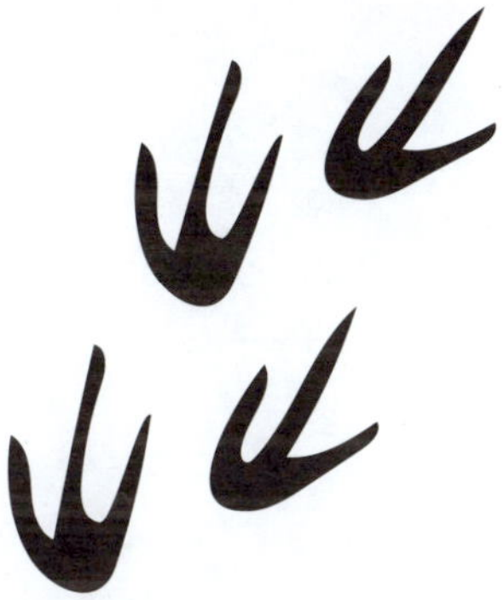

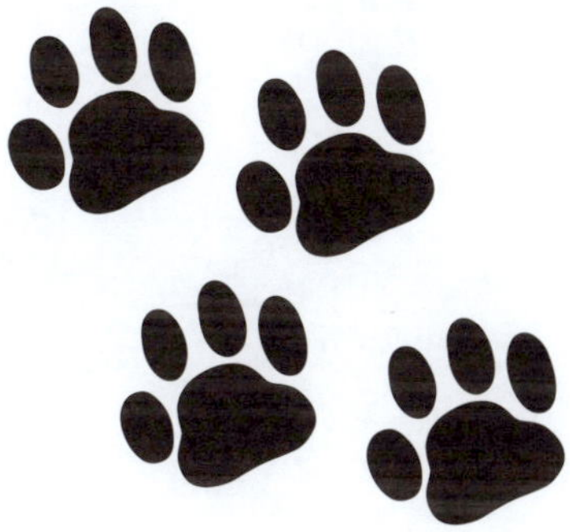

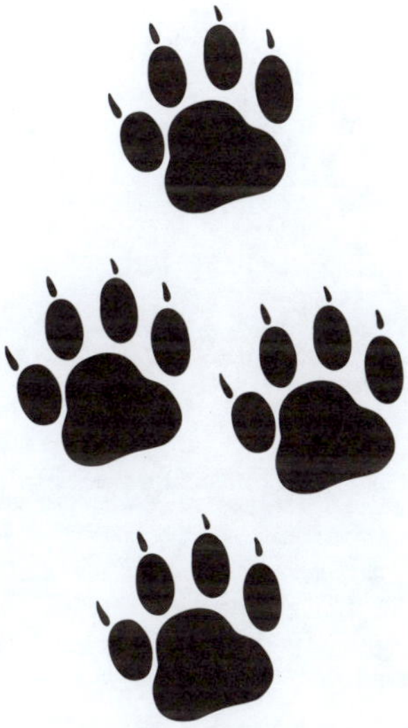

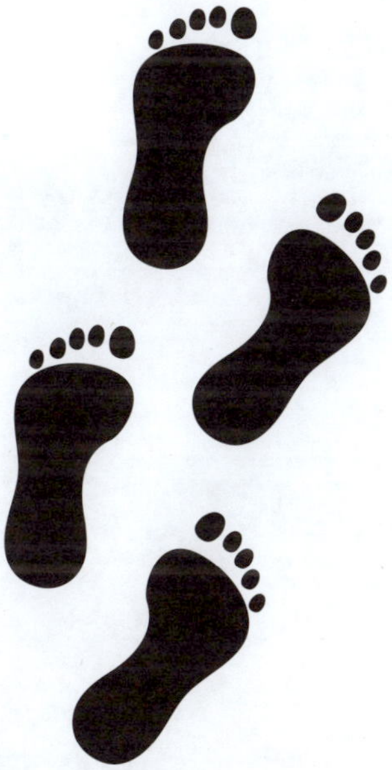

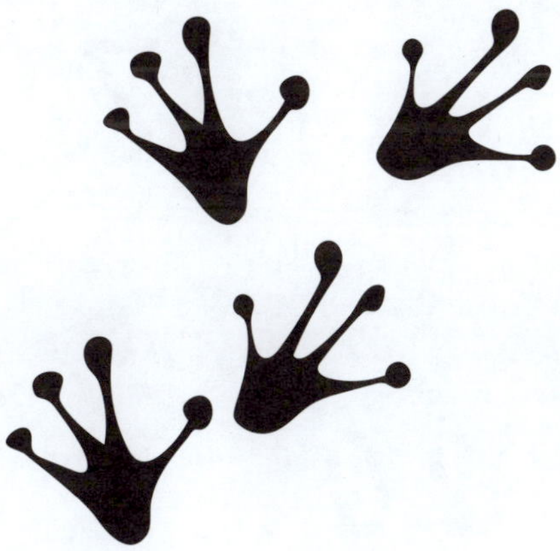

Numeracy

Connect the numbers from 1 to 20

1 3 4

2 5

7

6

10 8

9 14

13

11 12

15

18

17

16

19 20

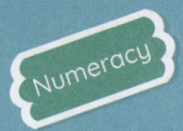

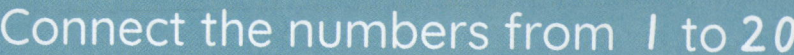

Literacy

Trace the letters a - z

a b c d

e f g h

i j k l

m n o p

q r s t

u v w x

y z

Identify and circle all the means of land transport

EVS

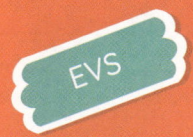

Circle the vegetables that grow under the soil

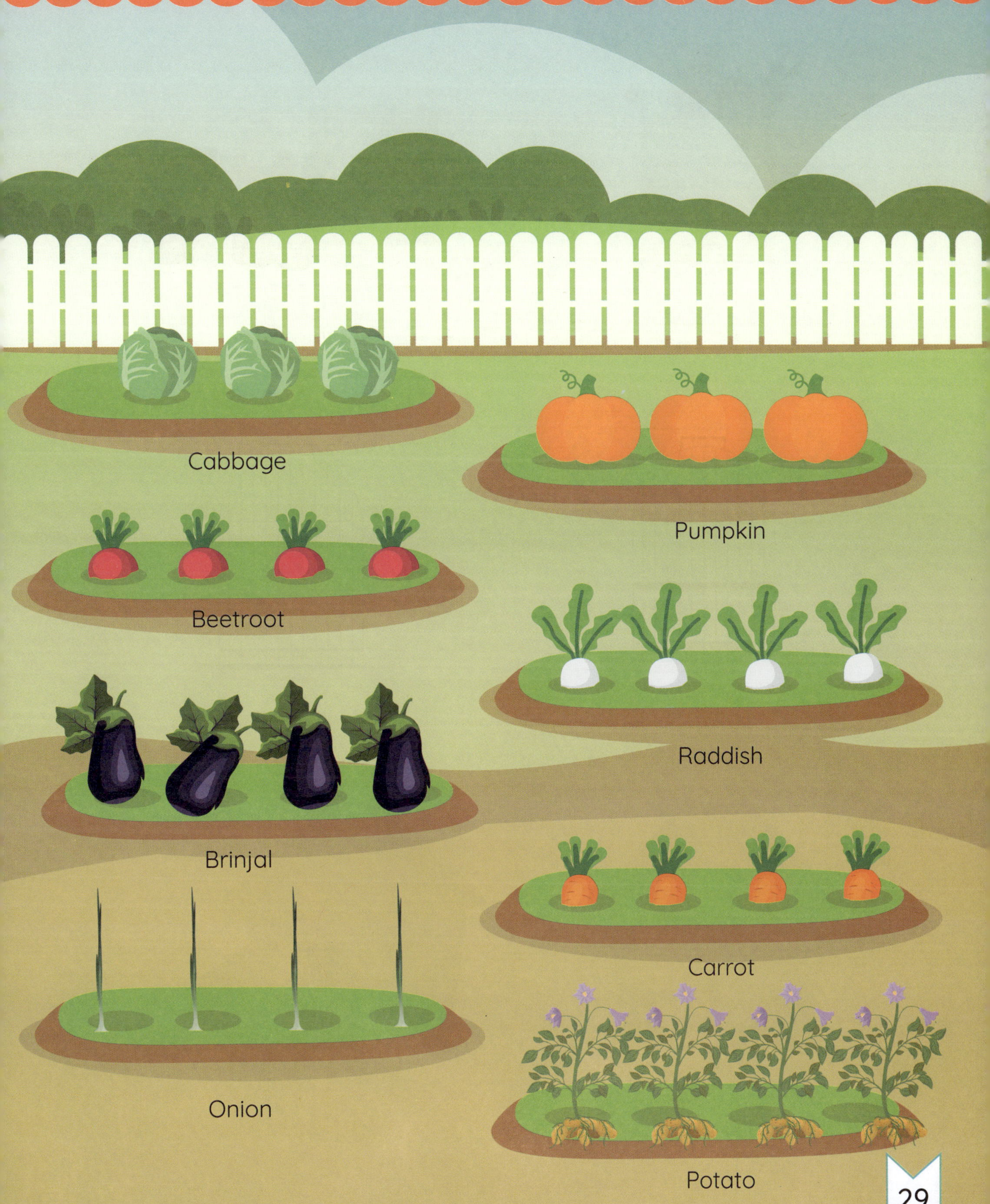
Cabbage
Pumpkin
Beetroot
Raddish
Brinjal
Carrot
Onion
Potato

Pre-math

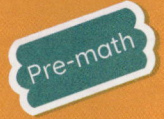

Mark pictures with objects inside with a tick, and pictures with objects outside with a cross

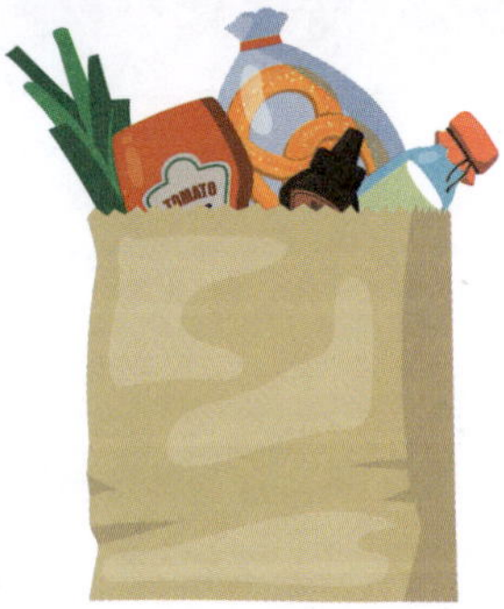

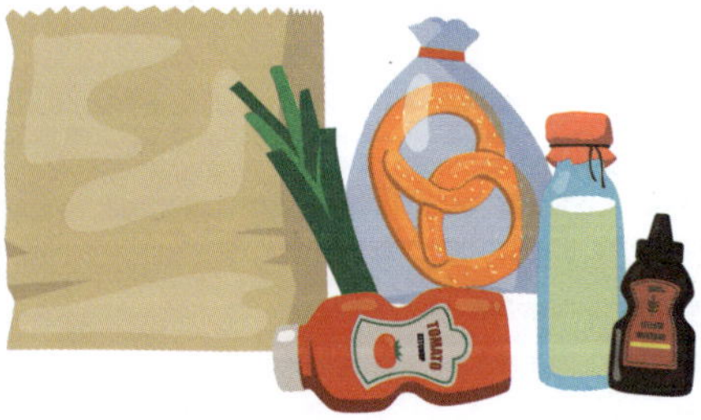

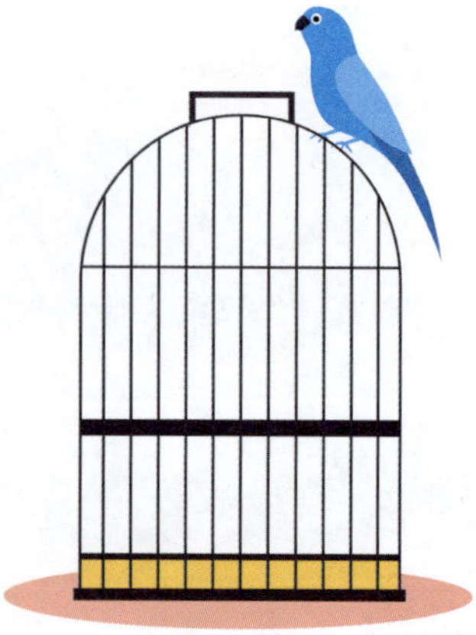

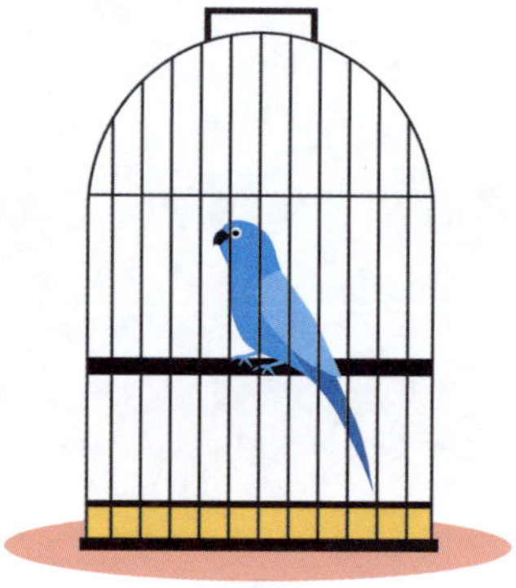

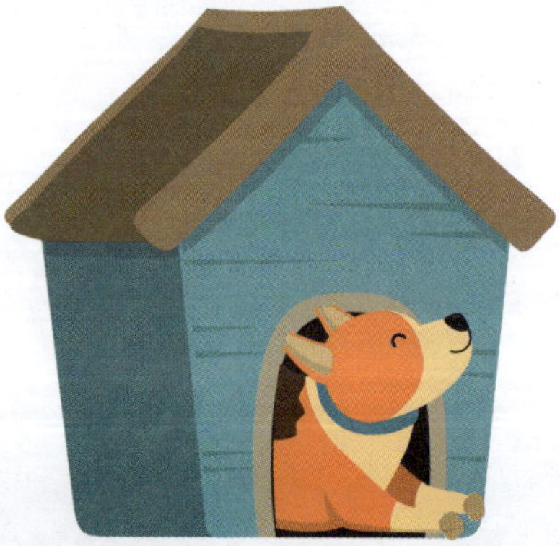

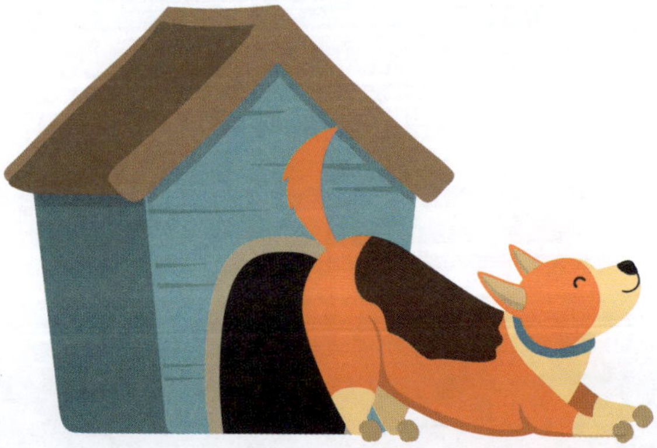

Trace the patterns

G

N

H

E

Help the animals reach their homes

Monkey

Worm

Bee

Lion

Dog

Aa Bb Cc Dd

Ee Ff Gg Hh

Ii Jj Kk Ll

Mm Nn Oo Pp

Qq Rr Ss Tt

Uu Vv Ww Xx

Yy Zz

Match the animals to their correct shadows

Turtle

Octopus

Fish

Seahorse

Whale

Jellyfish

Circle the odd one out in each box

EVS

Match the community helpers with their tools

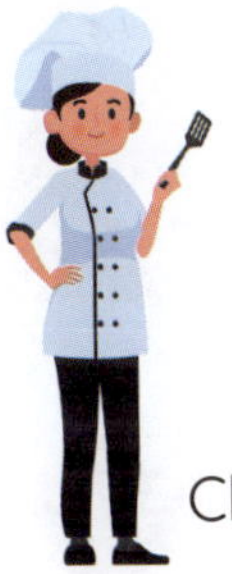

Chef

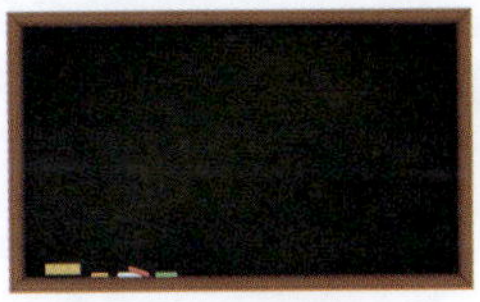

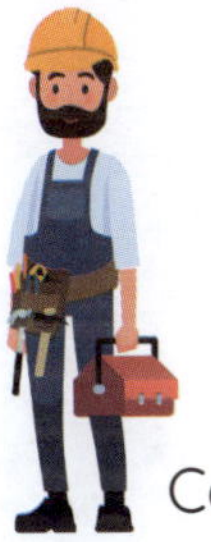

Carpenter

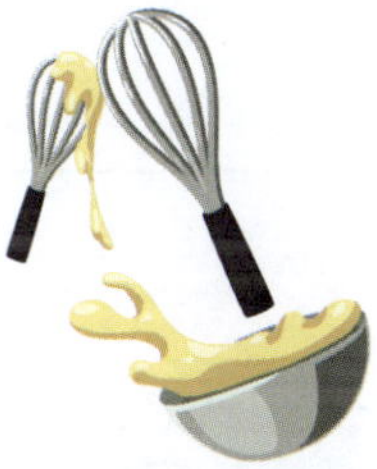

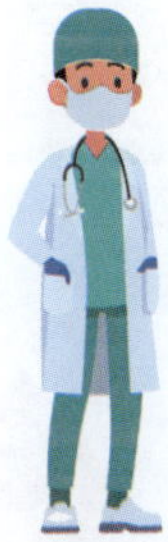

Doctor

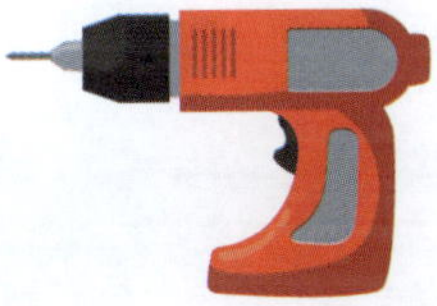

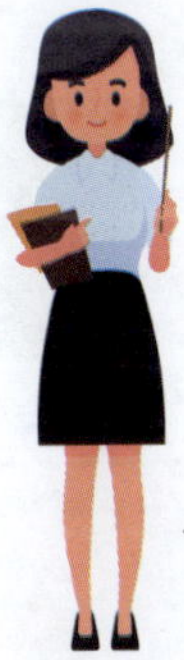

Teacher

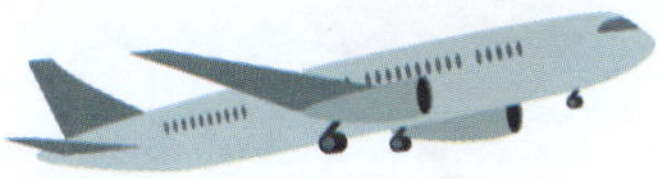

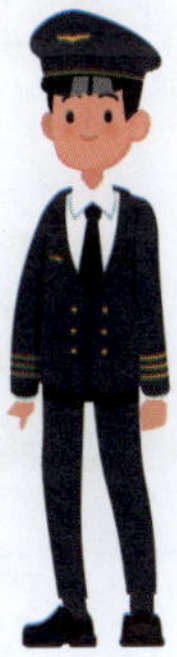

Pilot

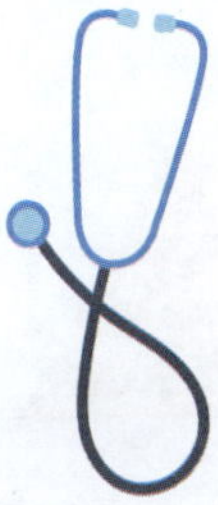

Observe the shape on the side and encircle the identical shape

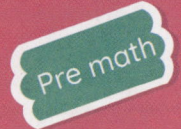

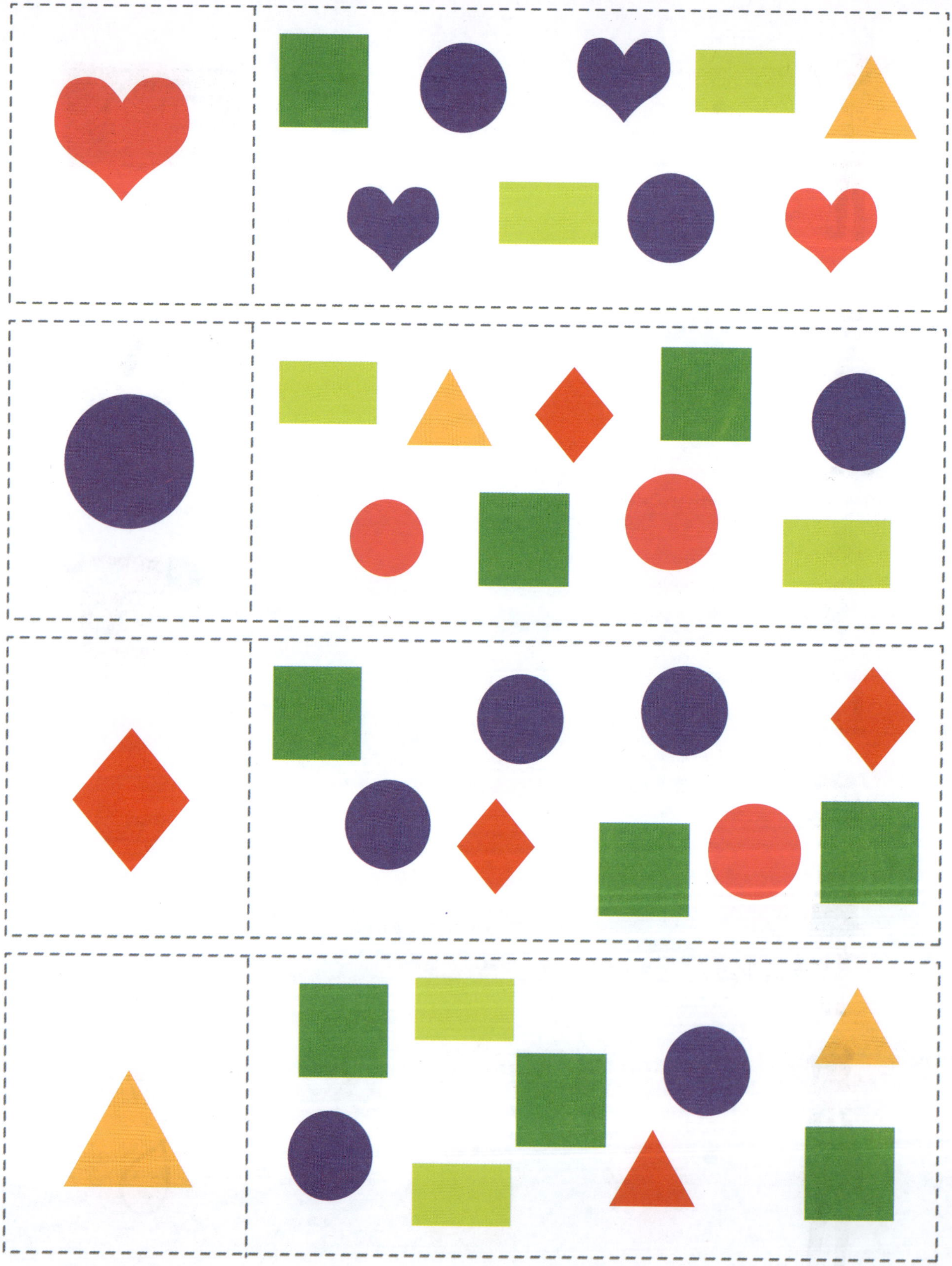

1 2 ☐ 4 ☐

11 ☐ 13 ☐ 15

5 ☐ 7 ☐ 9

☐ 16 17 ☐ ☐

☐ 17 ☐ 19 ☐

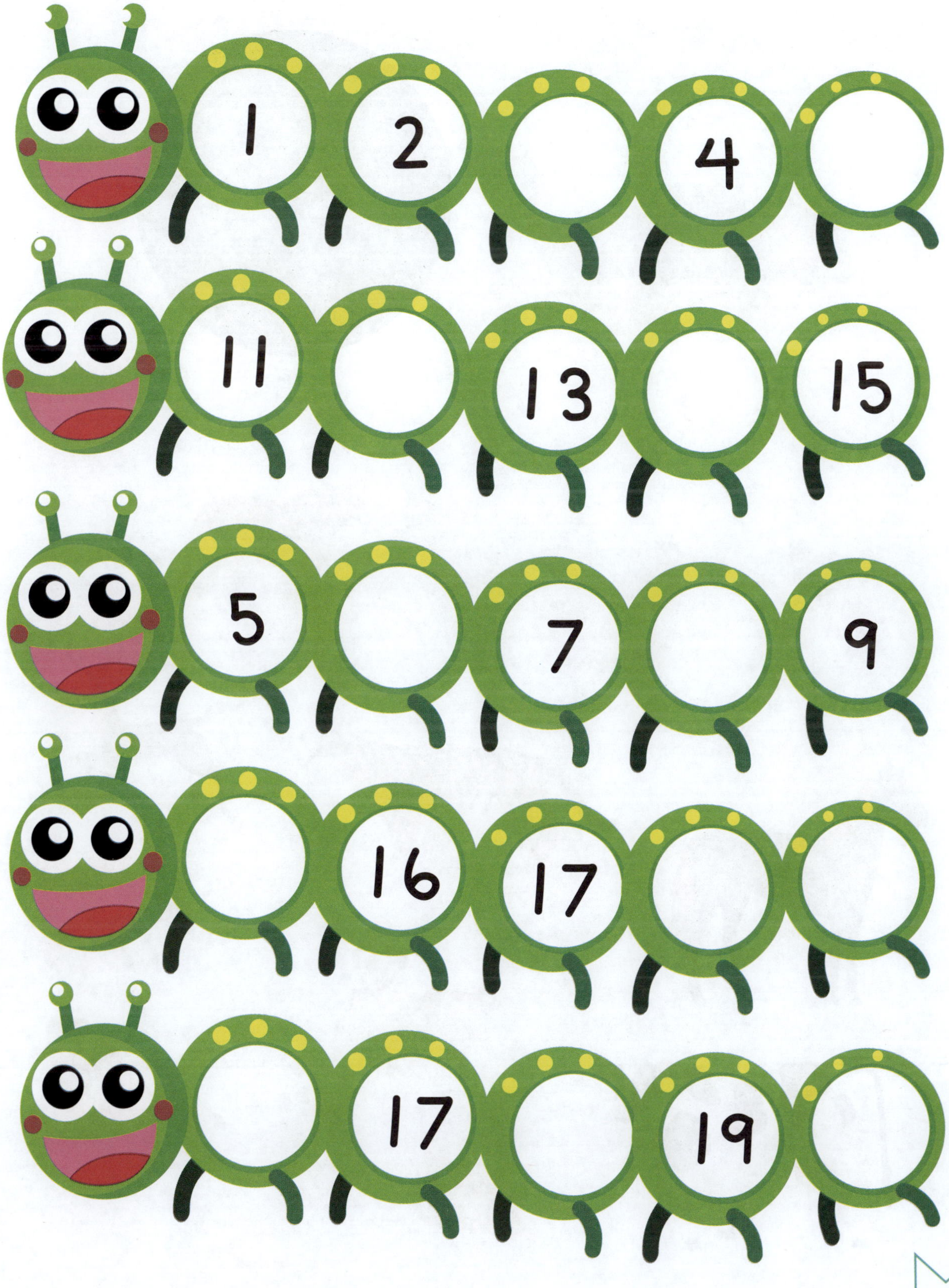

EVS

Pair the animals with their respective habitats

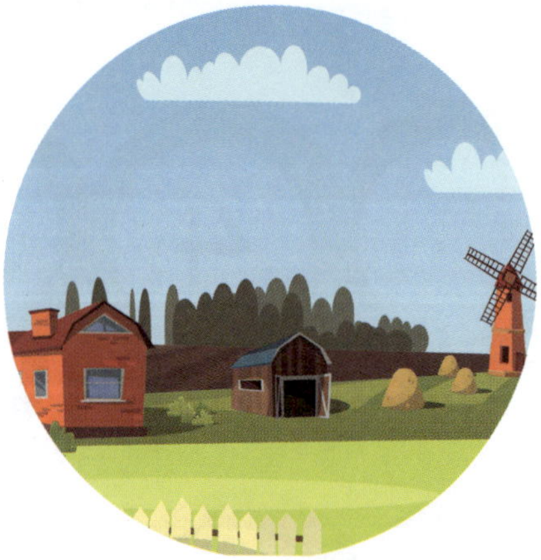

Farm

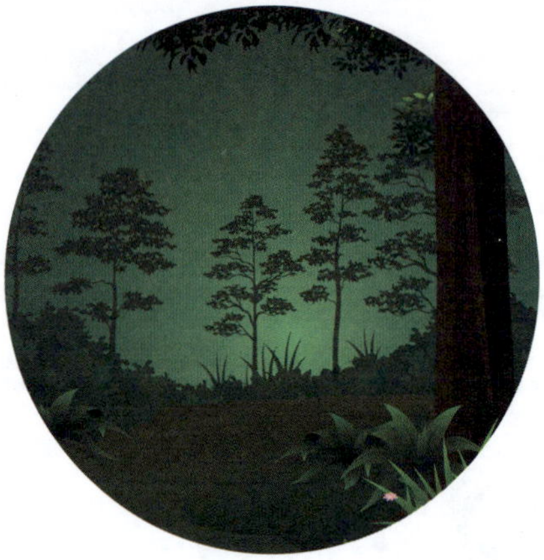

Forest

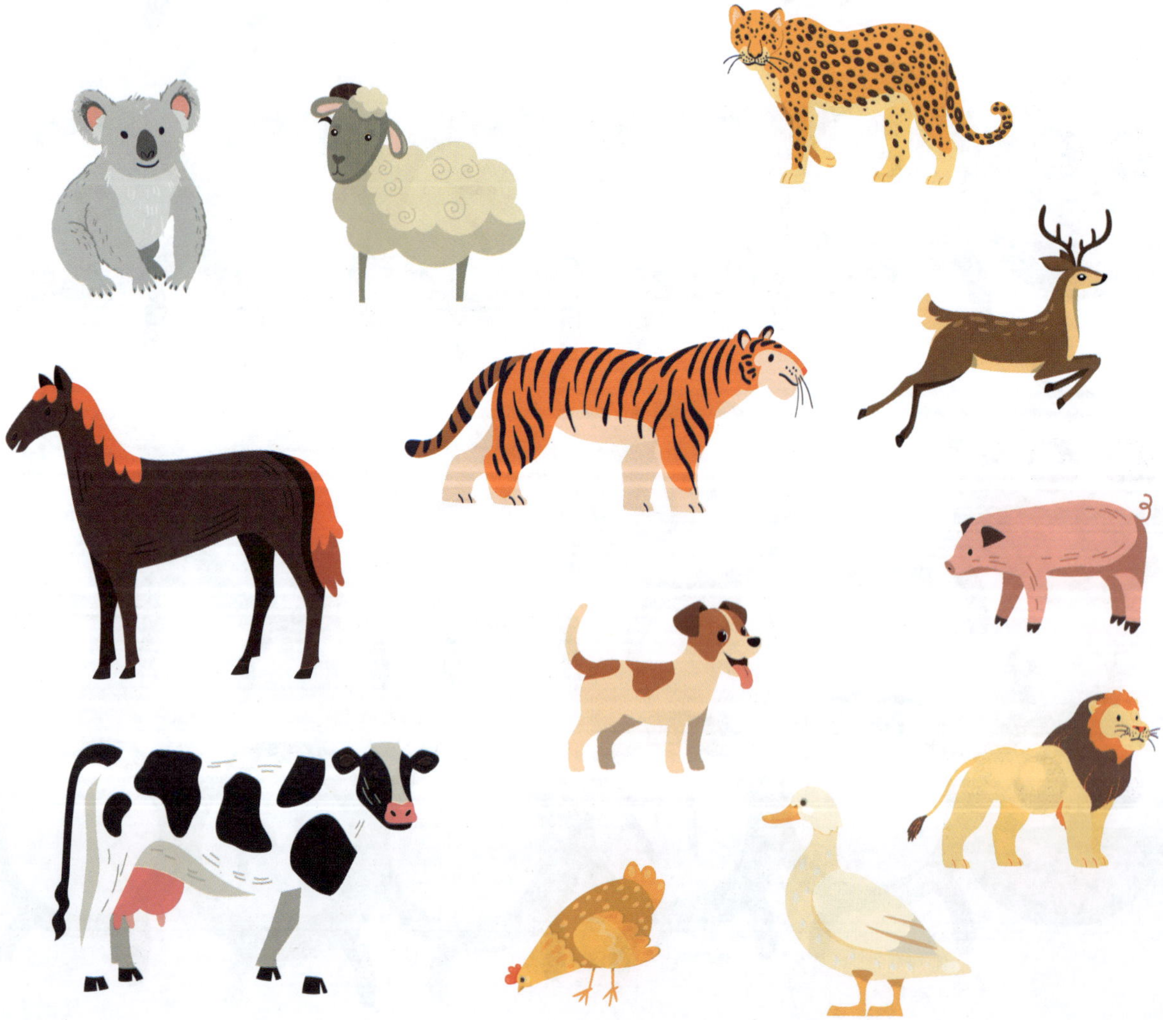

Literacy

Help the dog reach the kennel by completing the missing letters

Match the shadows to the appropriate vehicles

Aeroplane

Car

Scooter

Train

Bicycle

Boat

Rickshaw

Cognitive Development

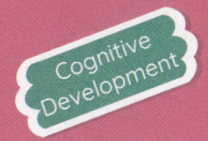

Examine the patterns and encircle the next item in the sequence

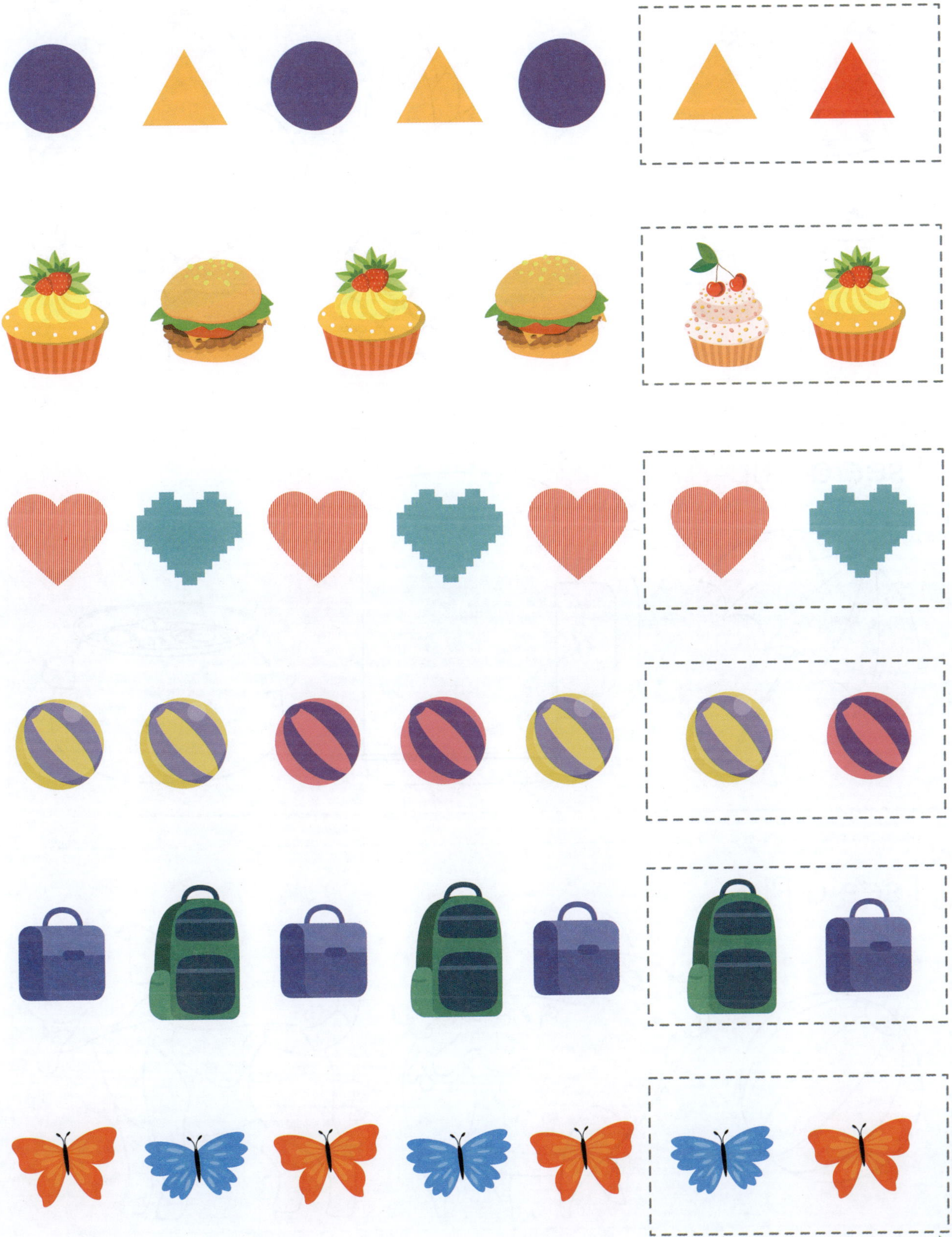

Colour as directed

I see a Tree

I see a Cup

I see a Pig

Cognitive Development

Colour the picture following the number codes

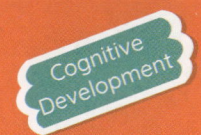

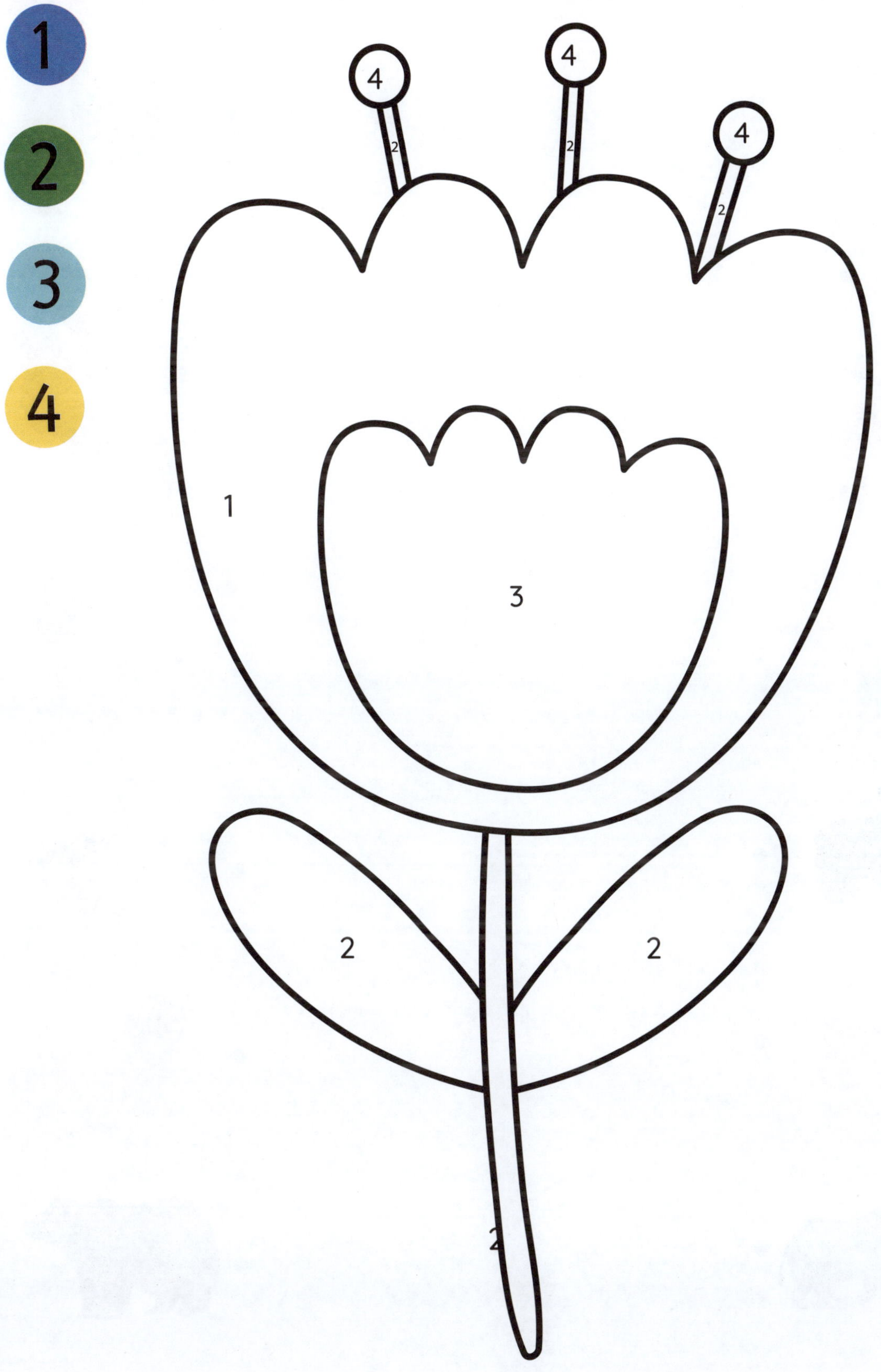

Match the young animals to their parents

Literacy

Fill in the missing letters

Aa ☐ Cc Dd

Ee Ff ☐ Hh

☐ Jj Kk Ll

Mm ☐ Oo Pp

Qq ☐ Ss Tt

☐ Vv Ww

Xx ☐ ☐

Cognitive Development

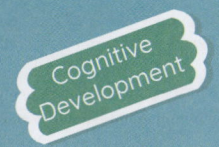

Match the pictures that go together

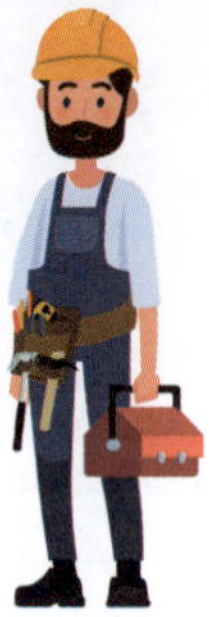

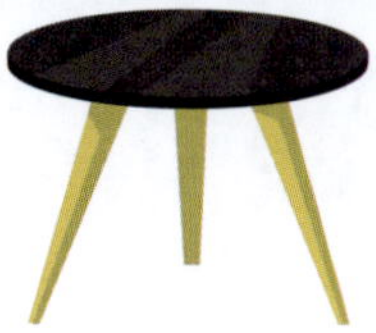

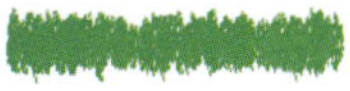

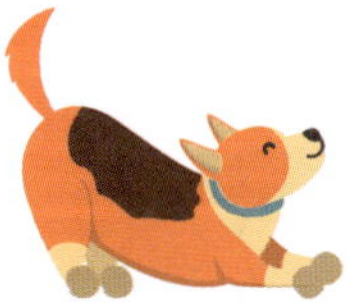

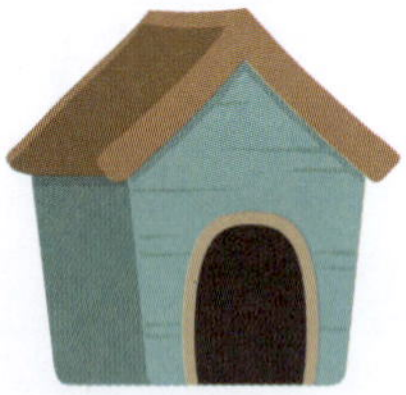

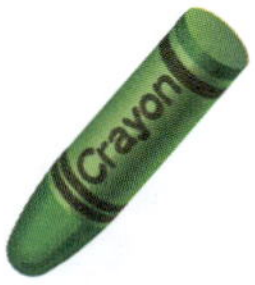

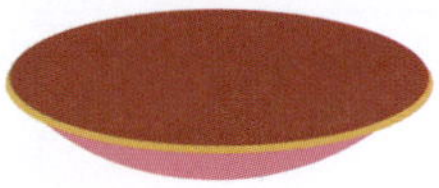

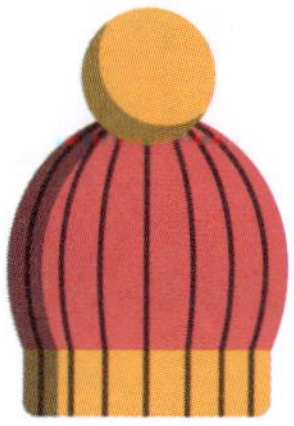

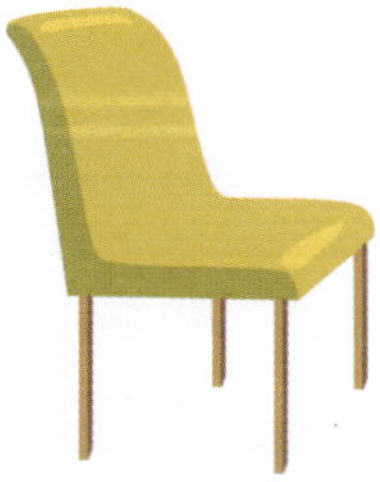

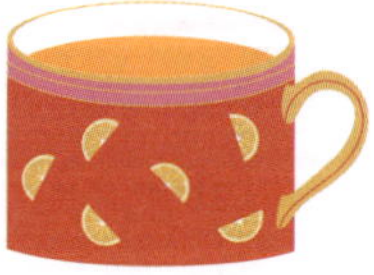

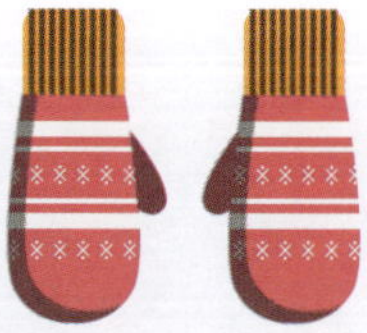

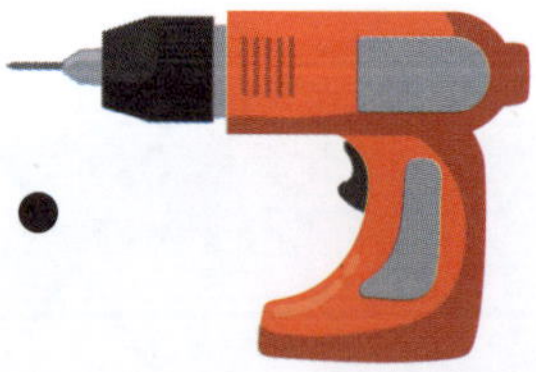

EVS

Circle the creature in each row that is the same as the one on the left

Jellyfish

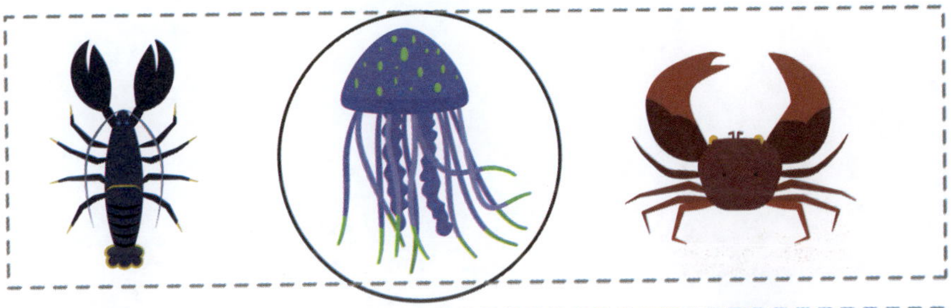

Dolphin

Fish

Crab

Scorpion

Seal

49

Pre-math

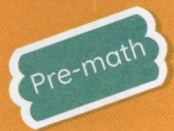

Observe the objects and match them to their correct shape

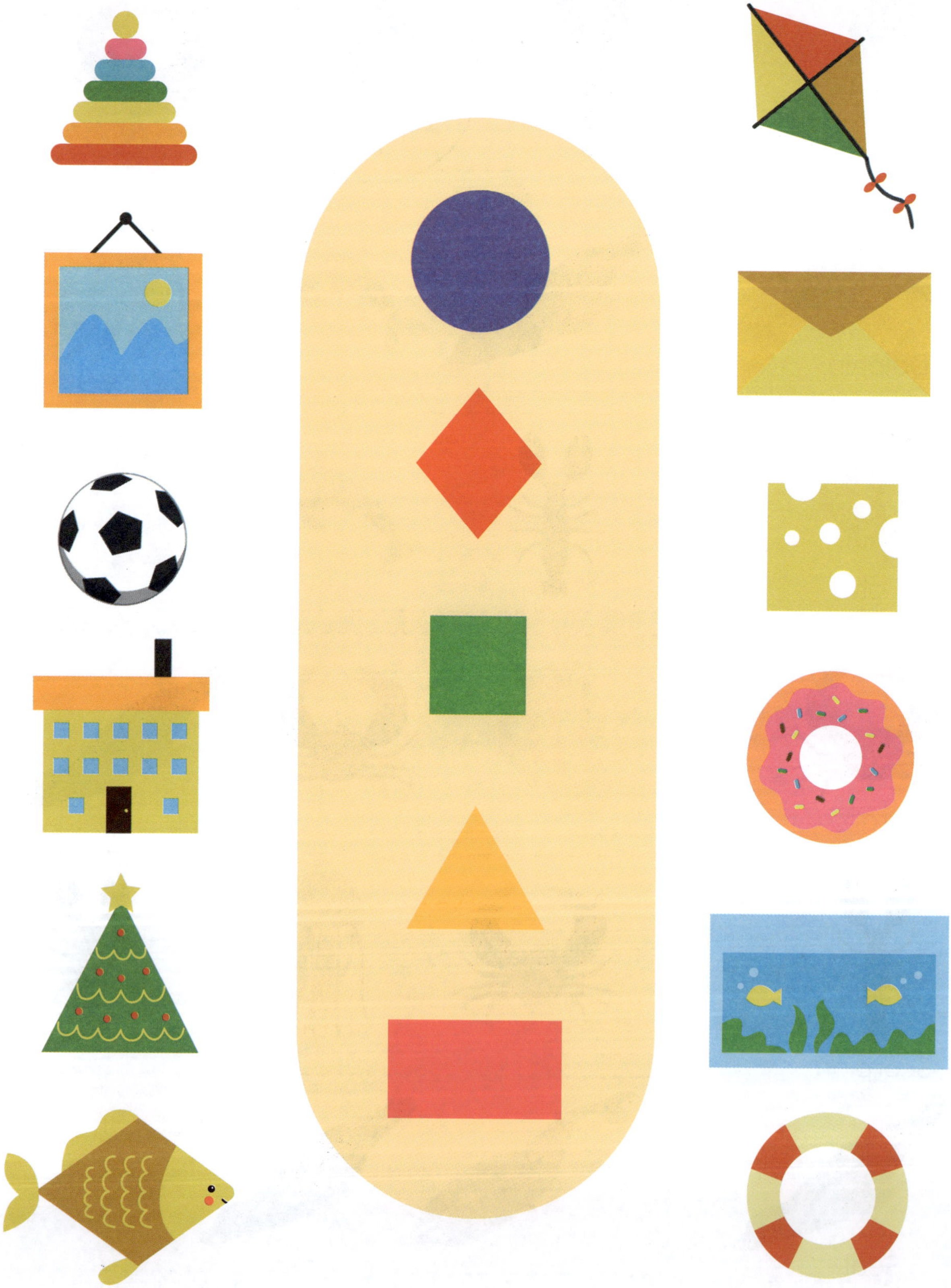

Pre-math

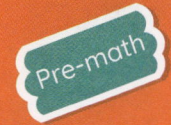

Bring out your colours and trace the shapes

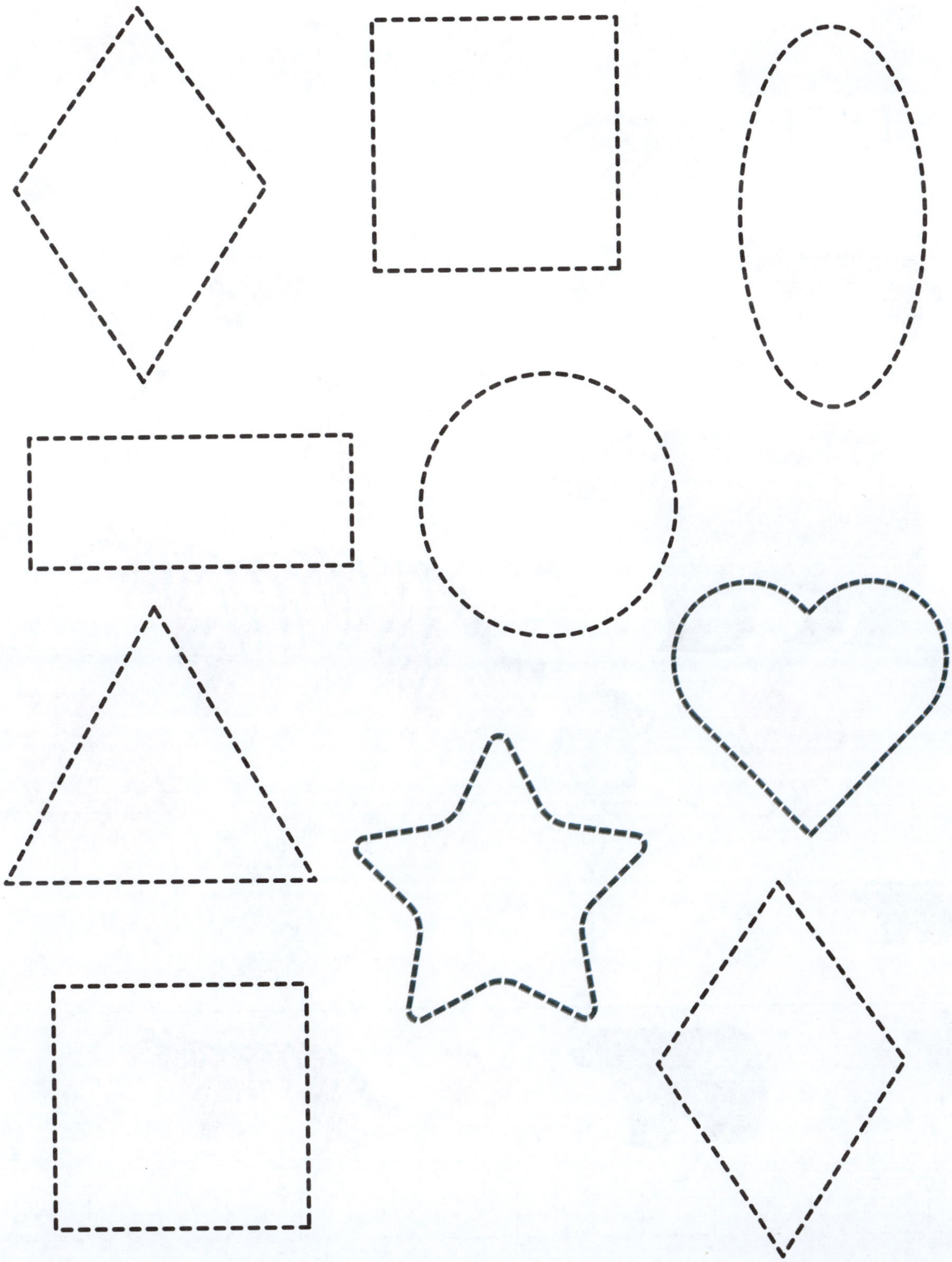

Numeracy

Count and write the number of animals and birds

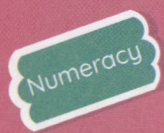

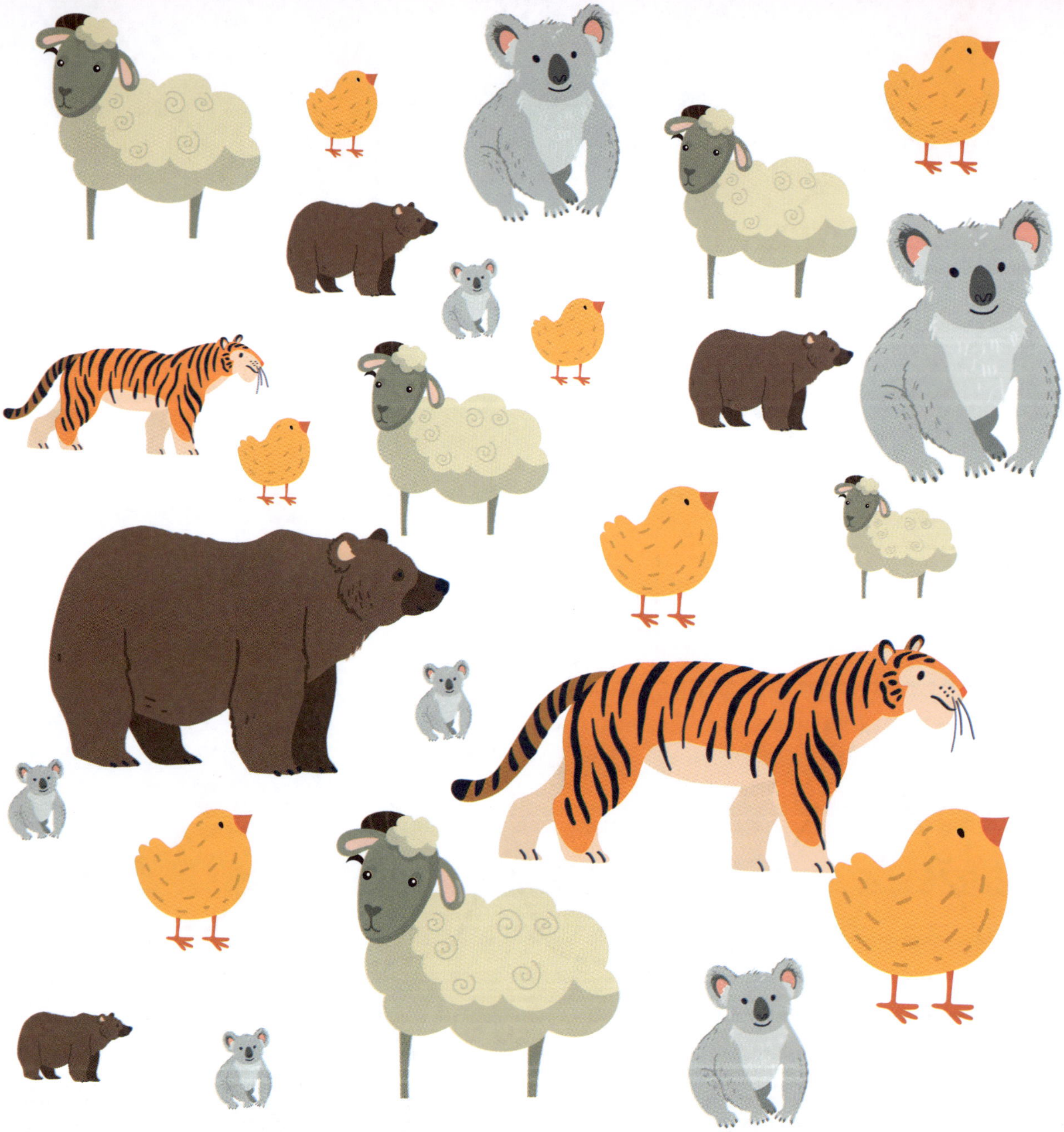

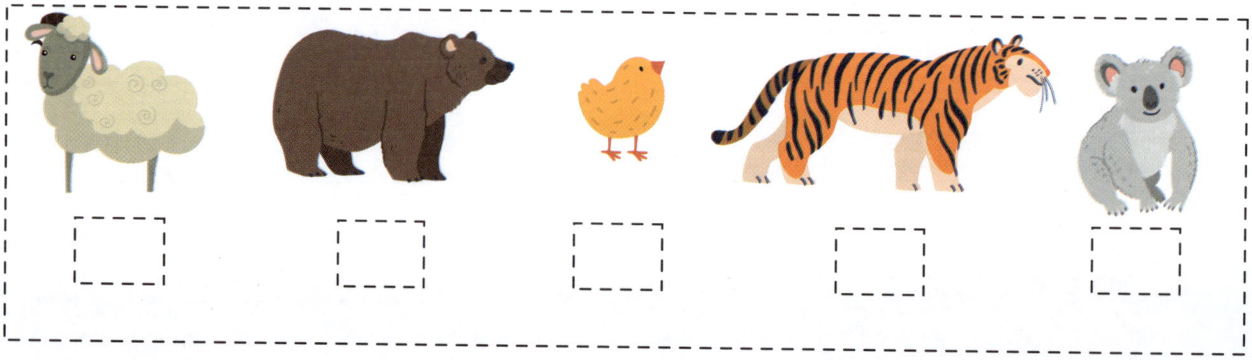

Identify and circle all the birds

Match each mode of transport to its corresponding vehicle

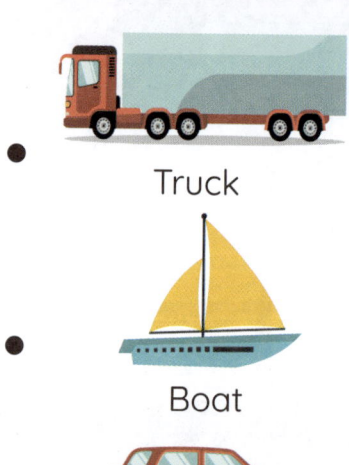
Truck

Boat

Car

Helicopter

Bus

Aeroplane

Van

Ship

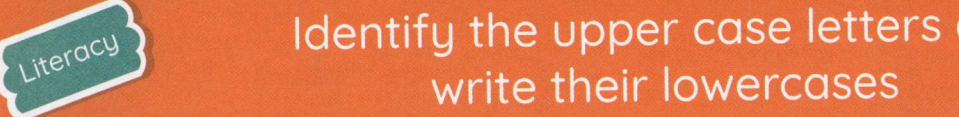

G _____

N _____

O _____

Q _____

X _____

C _____

E _____

V _____

D _____

F _____

P _____

L _____

T _____

S _____

A _____

W _____

B _____

R _____

Write the missing numbers

	2	3		
	7			10
		13		
16			19	
	22			25
26			29	

Match the animals to their shadows

Pre-math

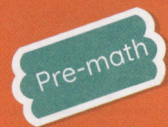

Count and circle the groups with less objects

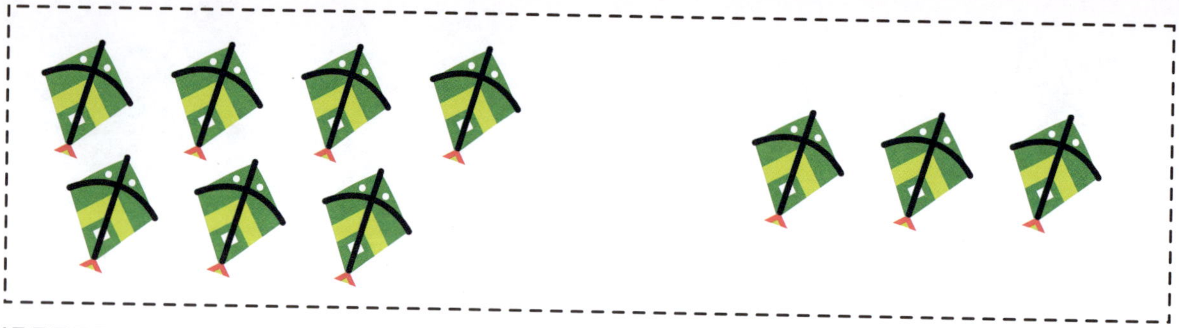

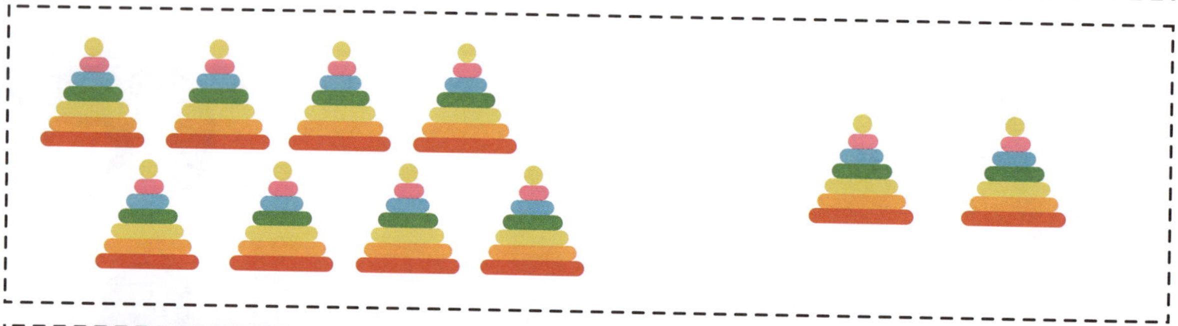

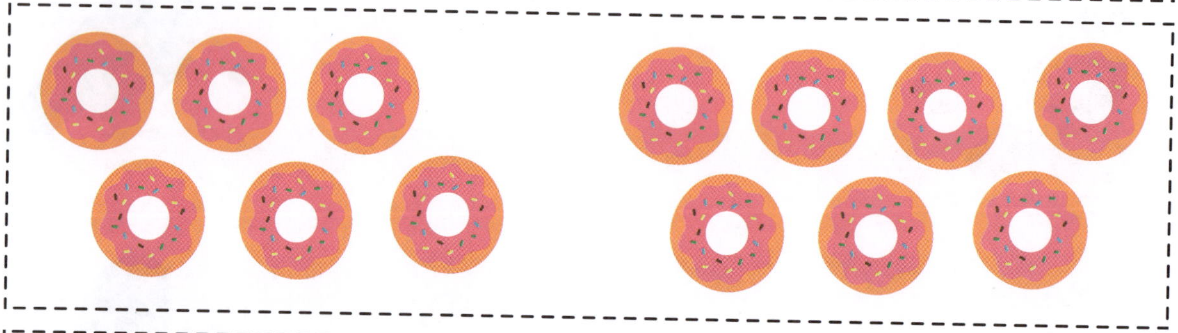

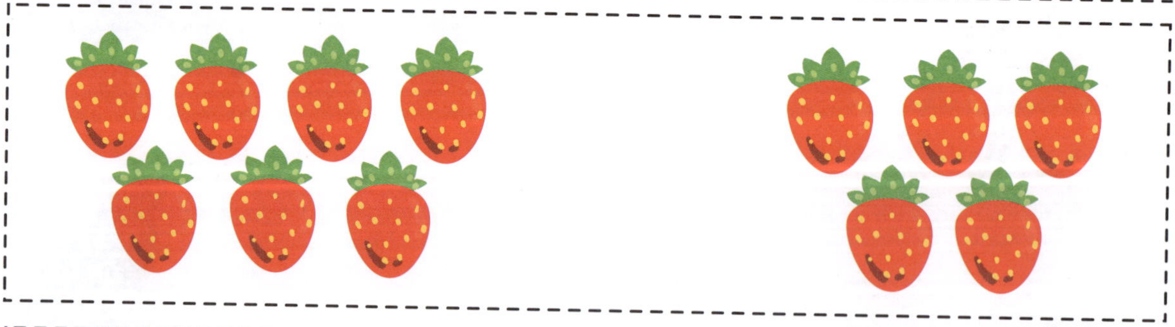

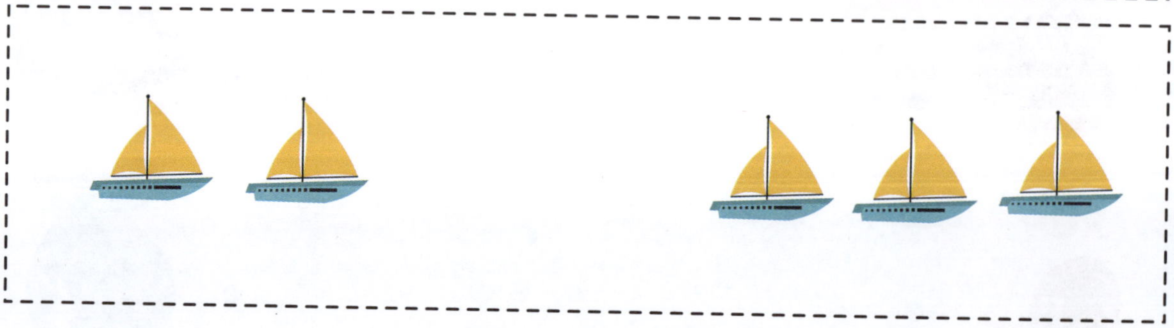

Numeracy

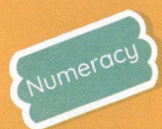

Count and write the number of aquatic animals

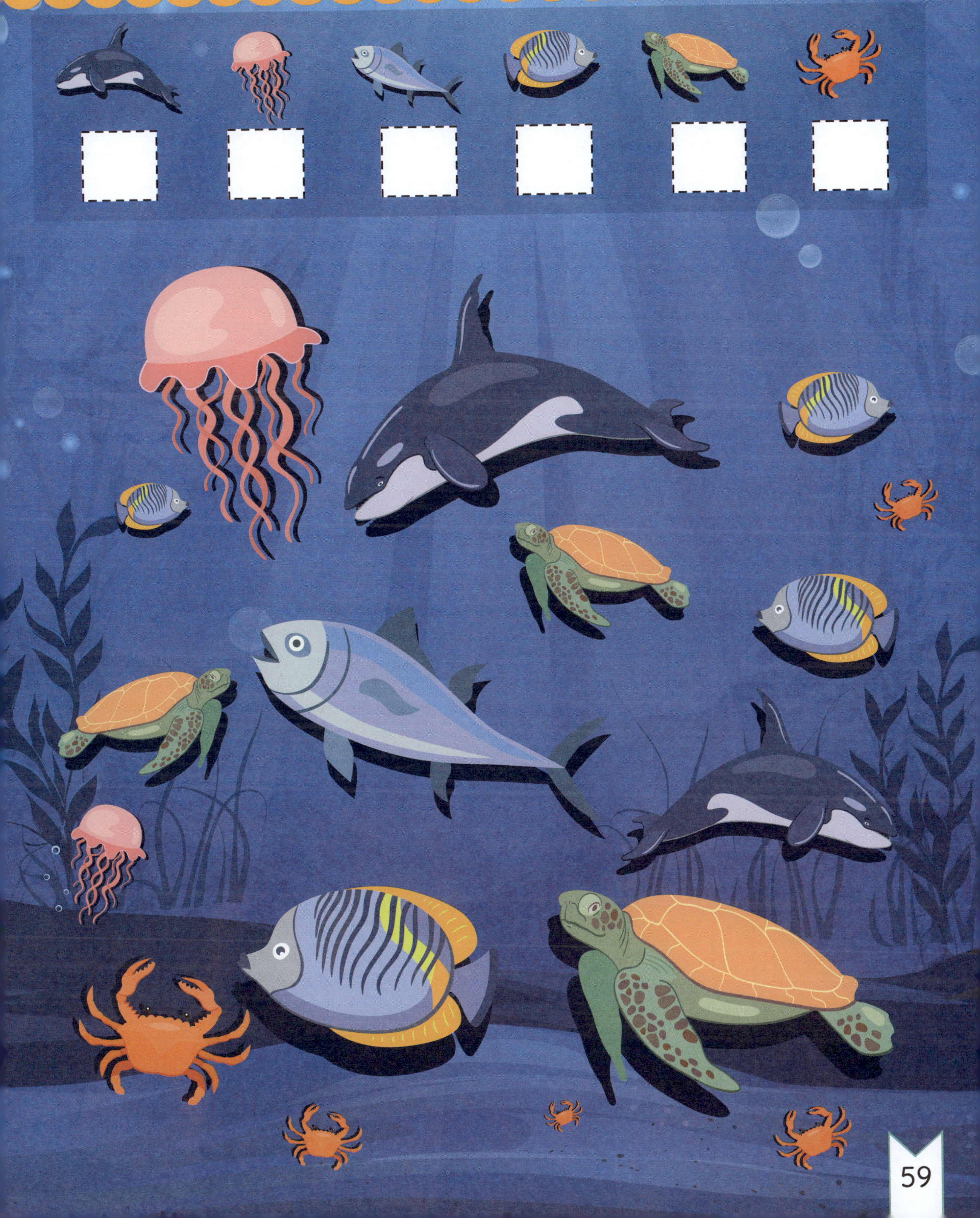

Complete the numbers 1-50

1	11	21	31	41
10				

Match the small animals with their big ones

bear

cat

dog

fish

turtle

snail

EVS

Write "F" for fruits and "V" for vegetables

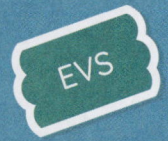

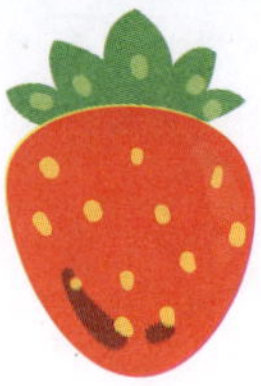
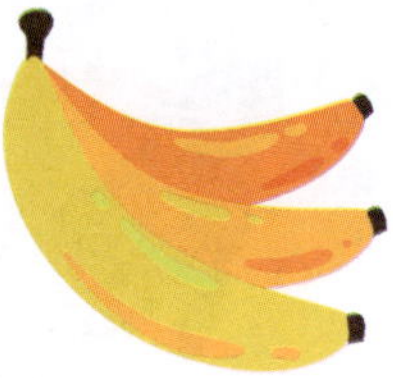
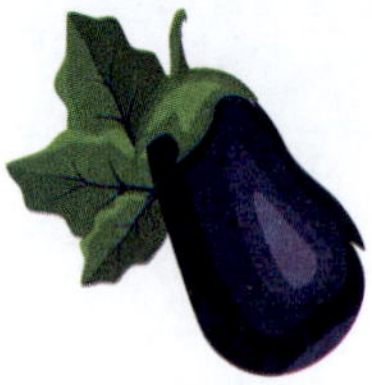
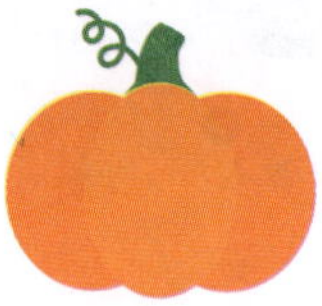
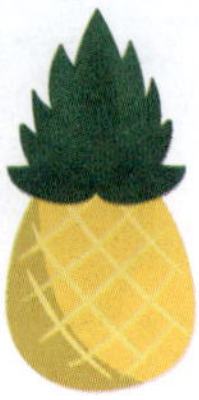

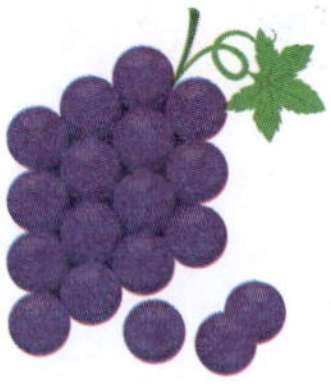
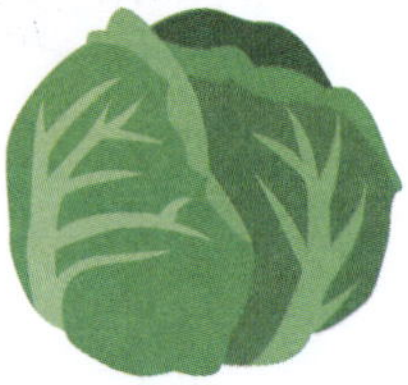
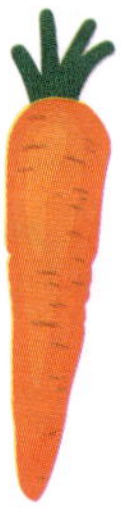
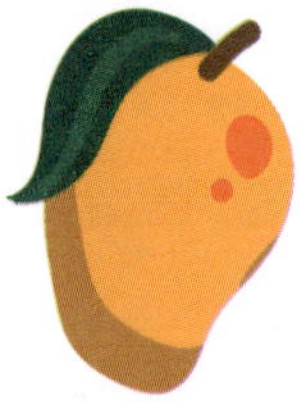
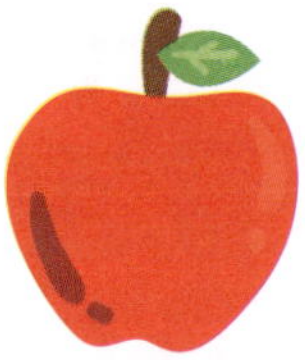

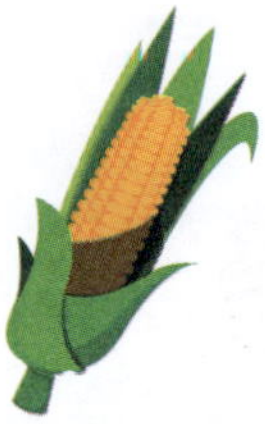
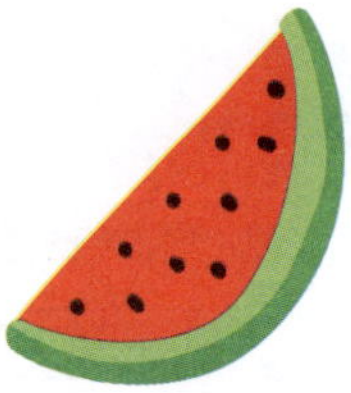
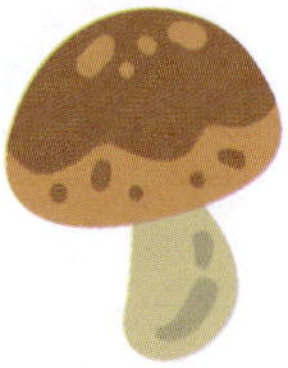
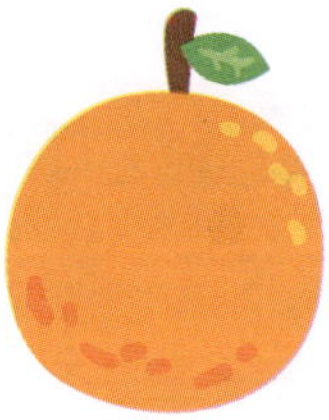
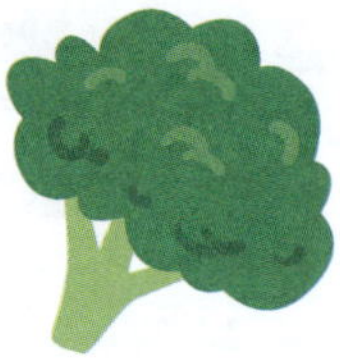

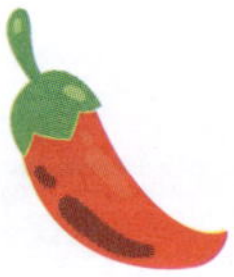
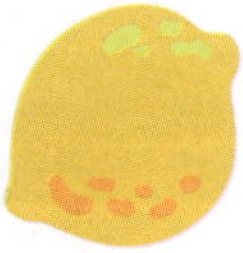
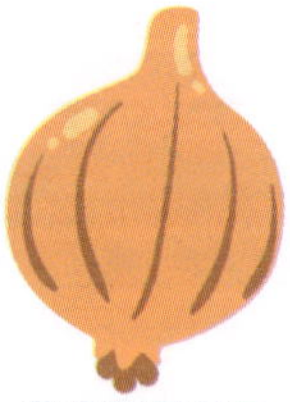
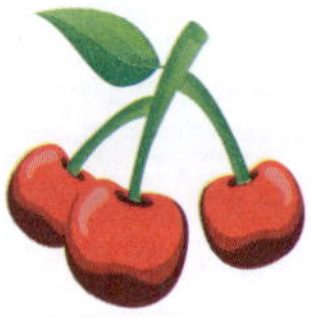
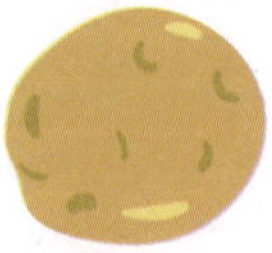

Circle the animals wearing glasses

ZOO

Match each animal with their favourite food

Rat

Cat

Squirrel

Monkey

Rabbit

EVS

Find and circle birds or animals that are on the ground

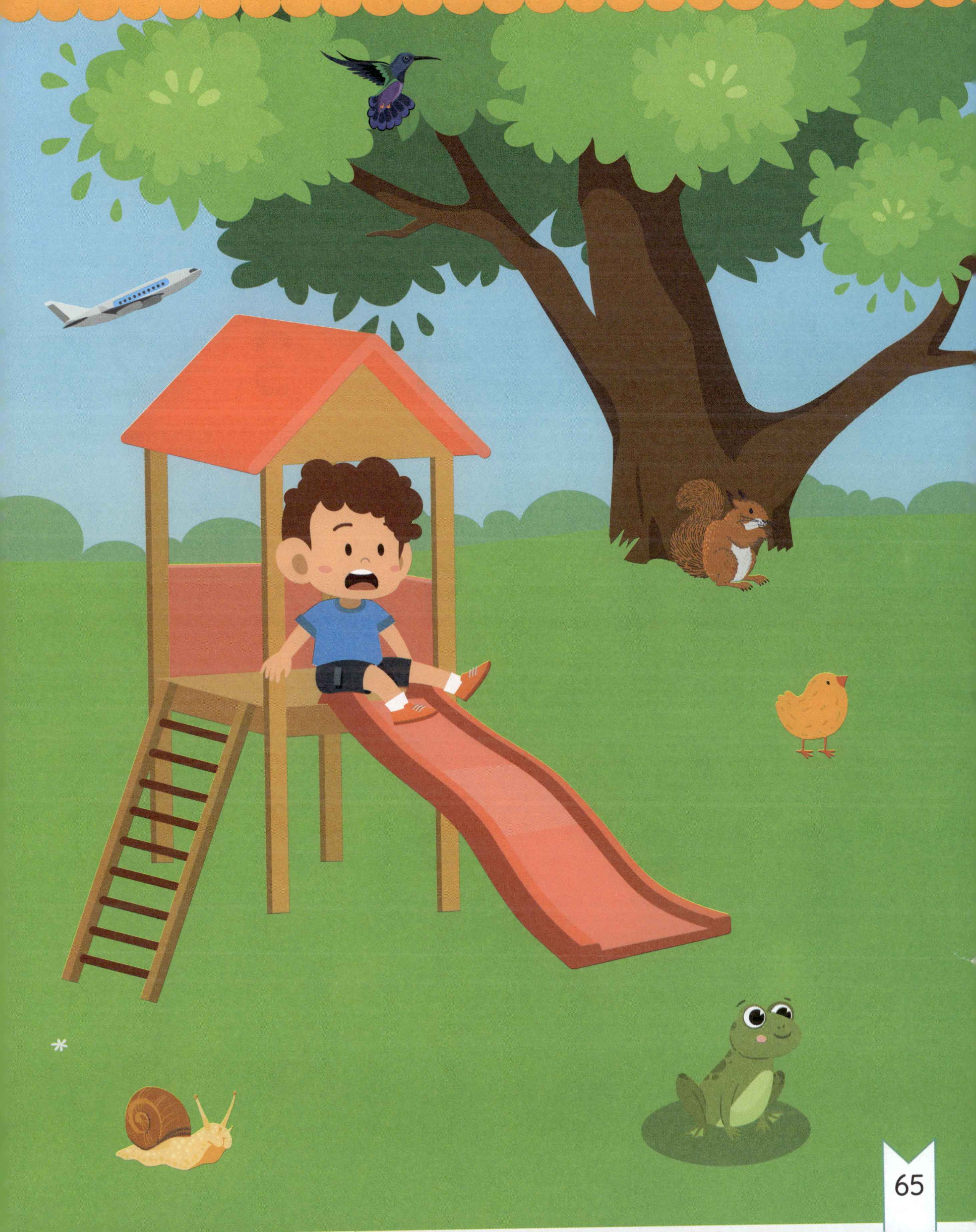

Count and circle

6   7   5

4   3   2

9   8   7

6   7   8

7   6   5

Match these animals' bodies to their faces

Goat

Hen

Elephant

Lion

Pig

Sheep

Bear

Cognitive Development

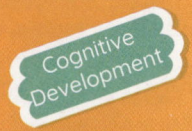

Circle the things which are placed outside the nest

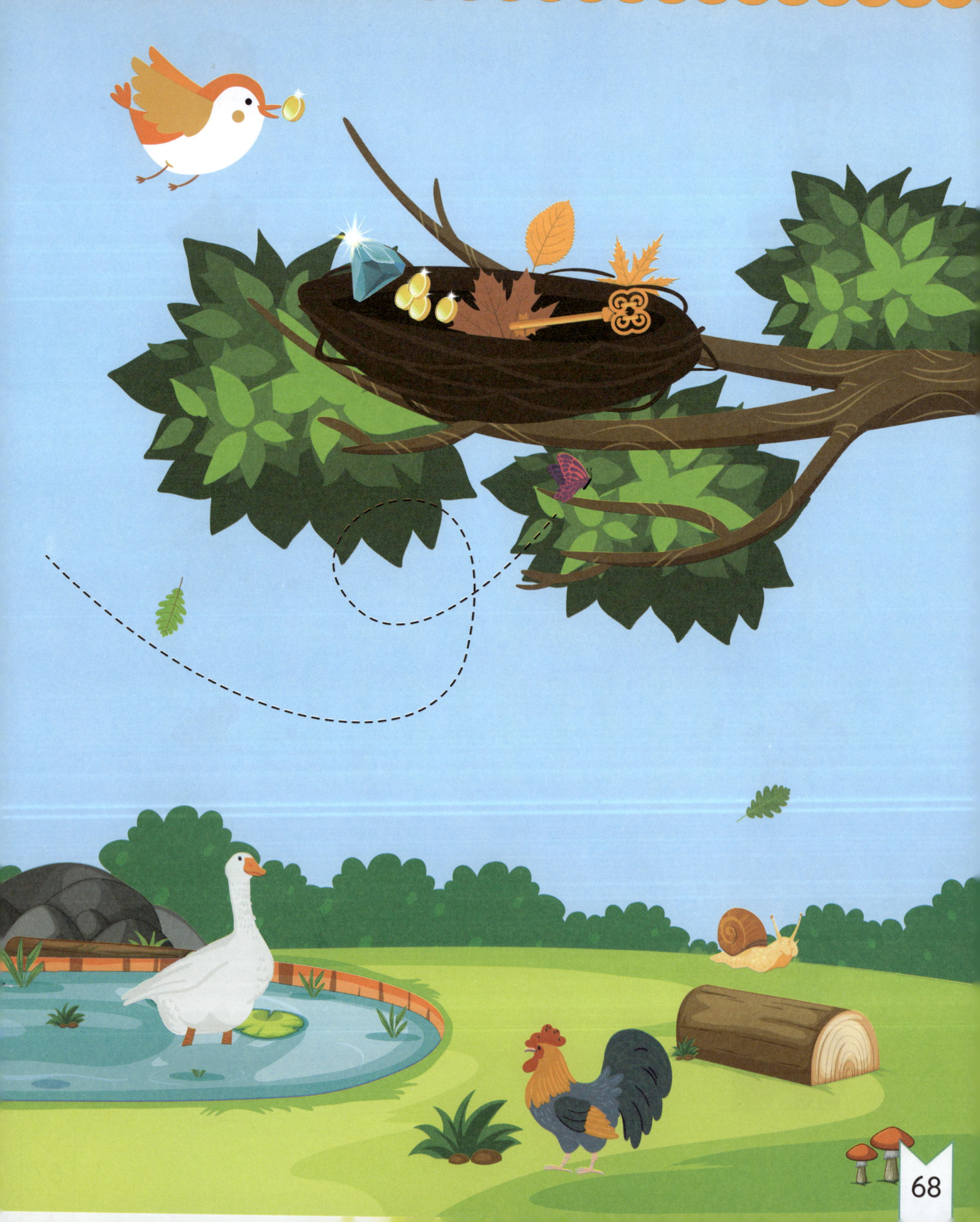

Help the bees reach the beehive
using the correct path A - Z

Numeracy

Count and write the number of similar fruits and vegetables

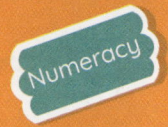

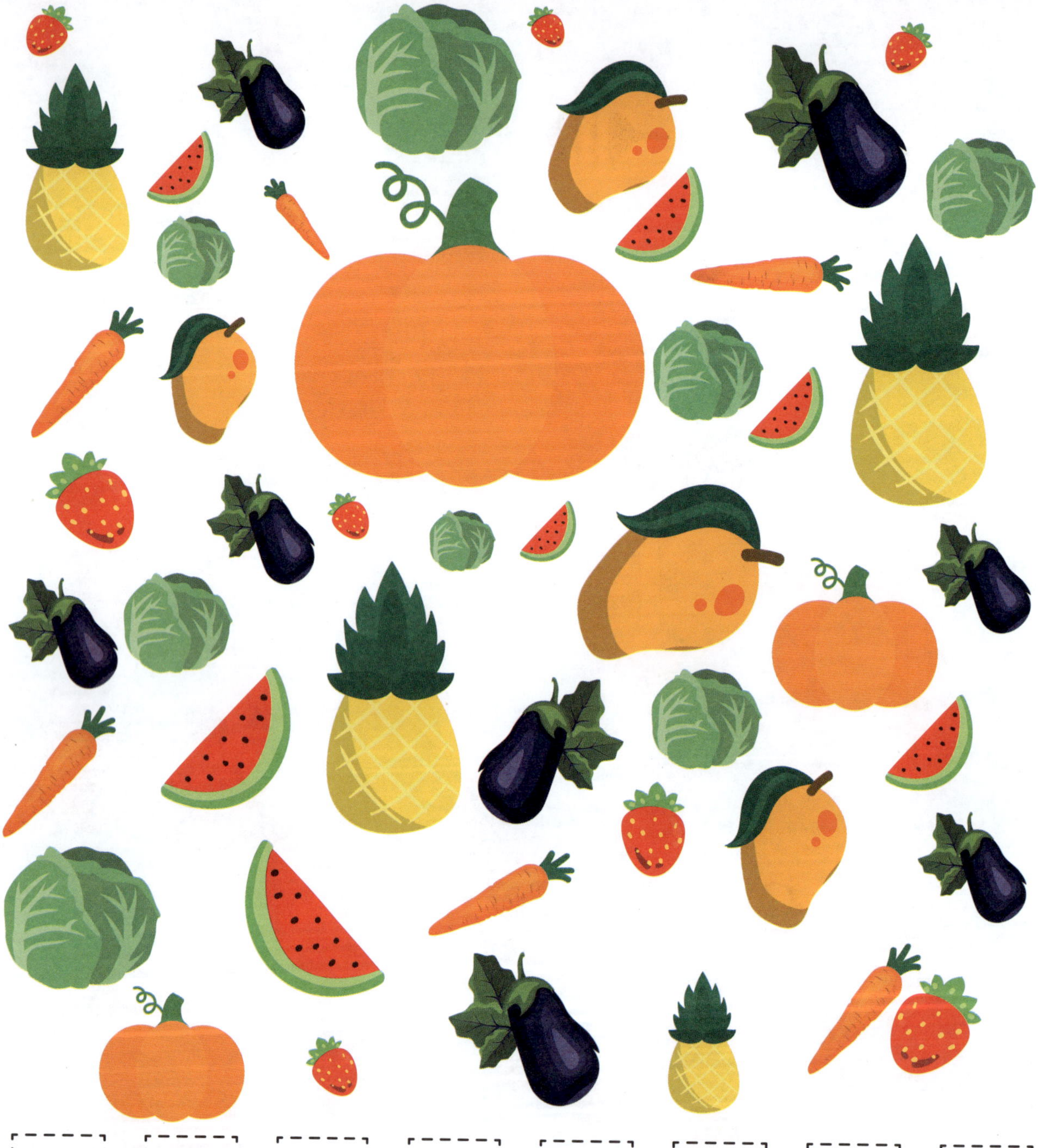

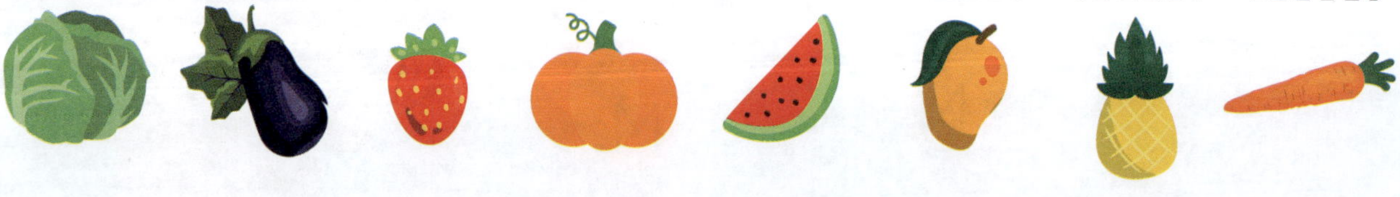

Match the vehicles to the direction they are travelling

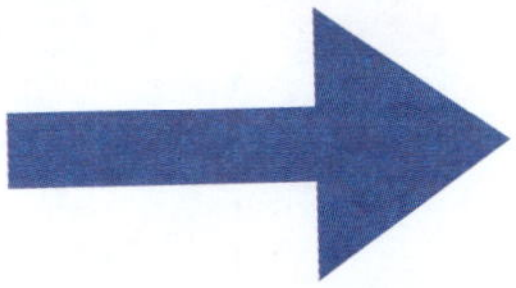

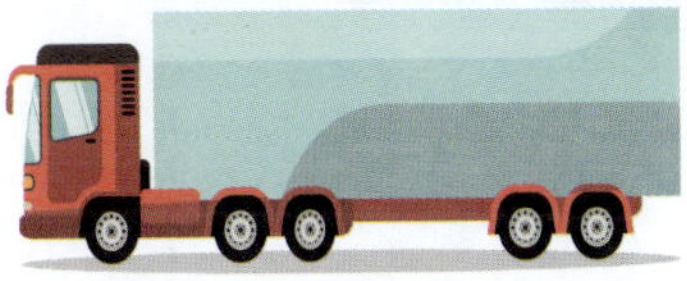

Truck

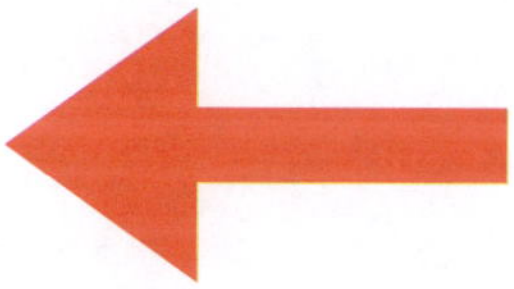

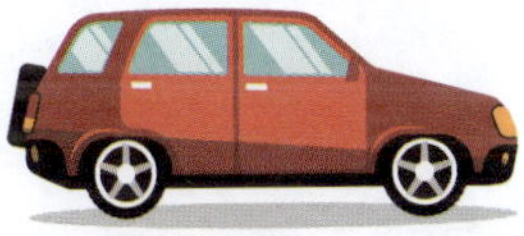

Car

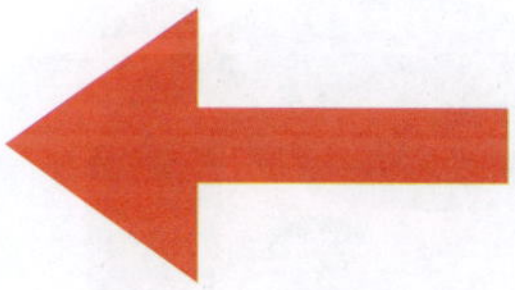

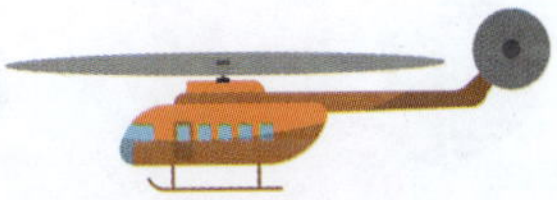

Helicopter

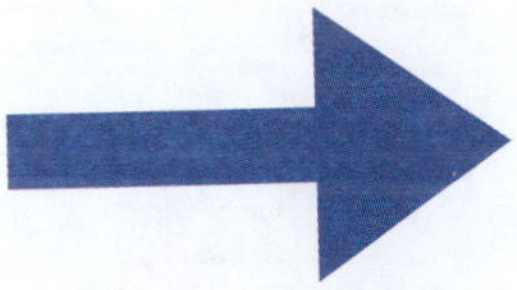

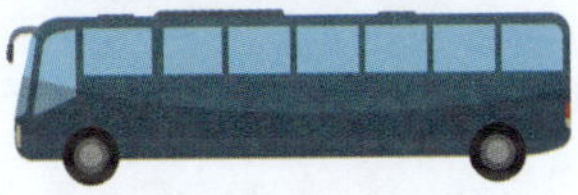

Bus

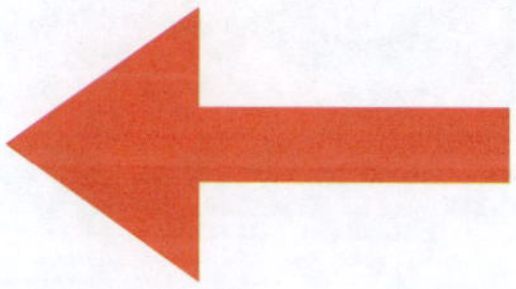

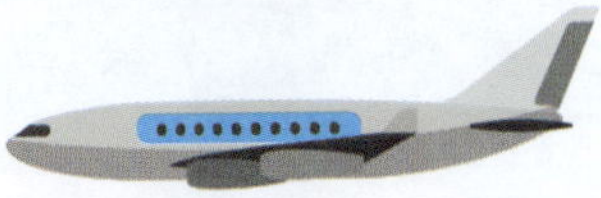

Aeroplane

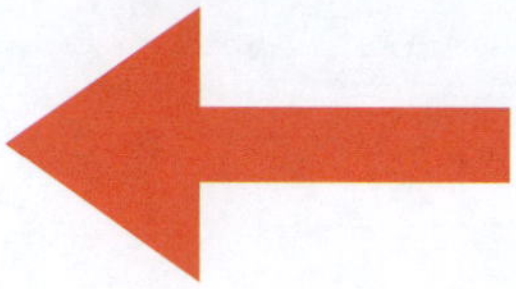

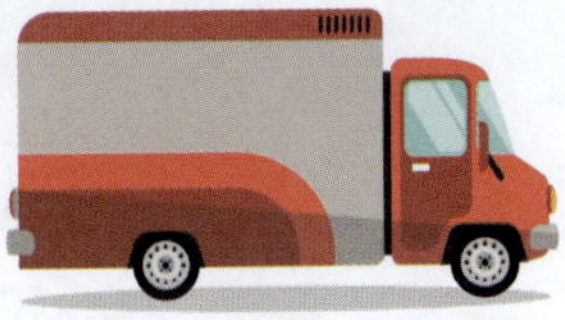

Van

71

Write the numbers that come after

8	9		15	
27			35	
42			40	
21			49	
2			32	
14			30	
20			9	

Match the animals to their pictures

Hen

Elephant

Lion

Pig

Sheep

Bear

Pre-math

Associate objects with their corresponding colours

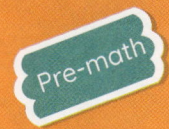

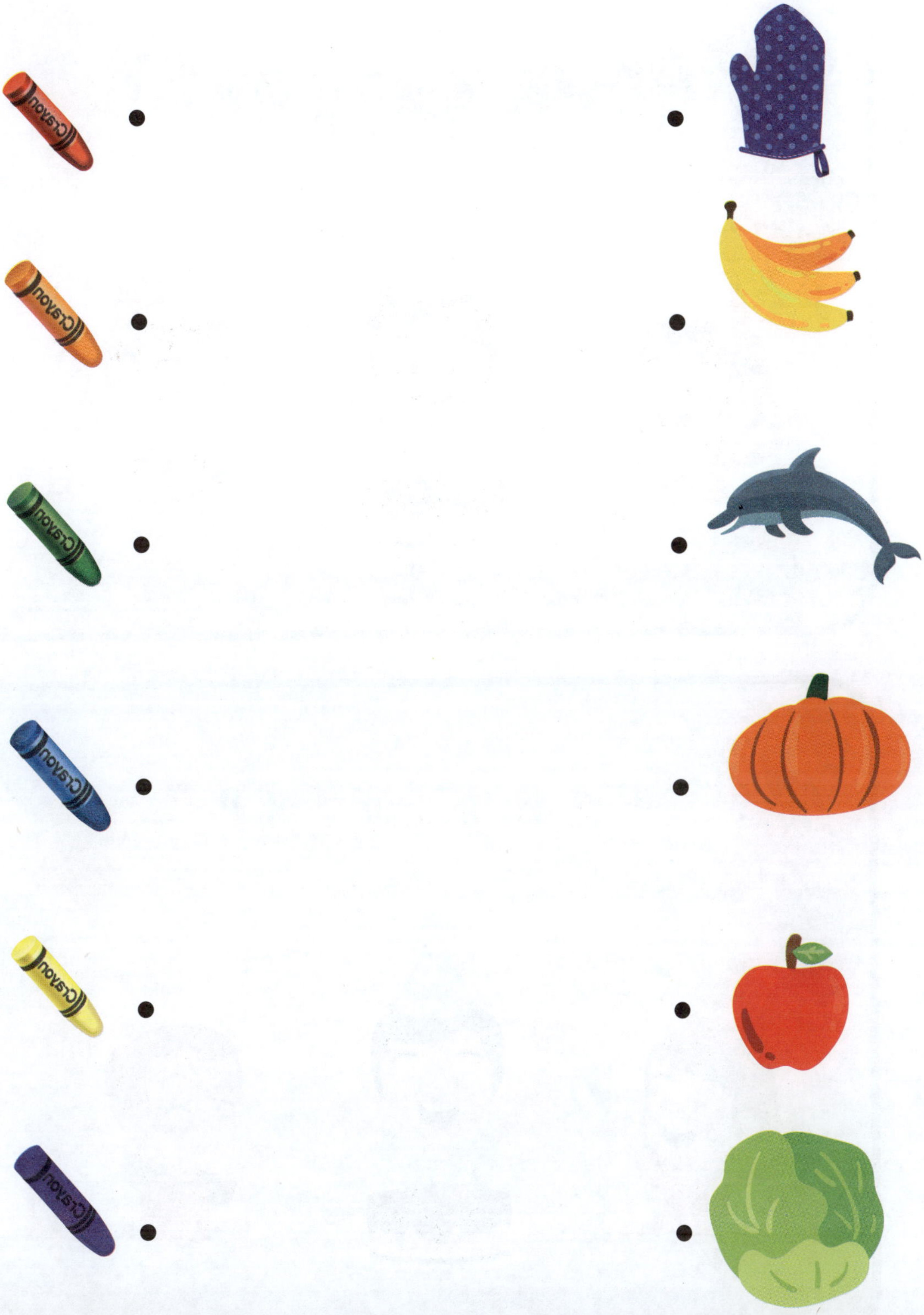

Spot and circle the differences in these birthday pictures

EVS

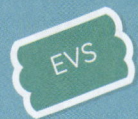

Match the birds with their respective shadows

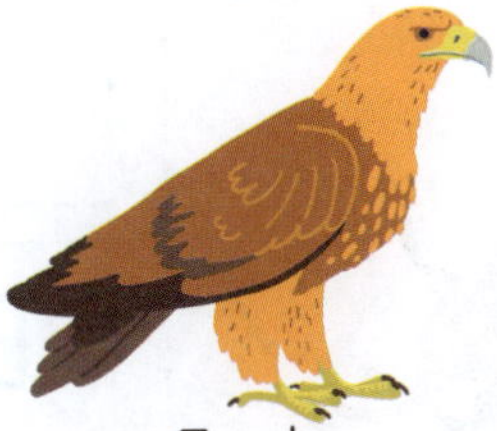
Eagle

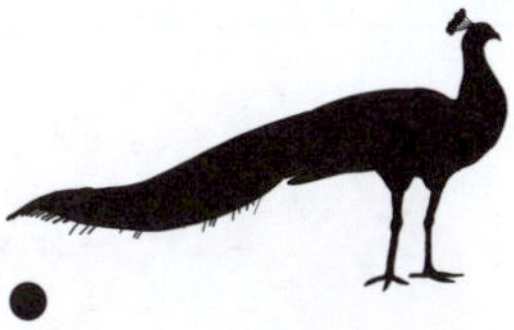

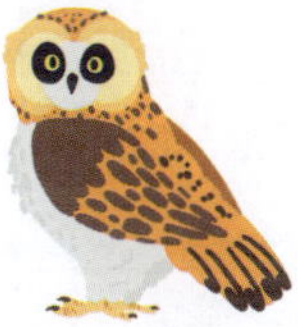
Owl

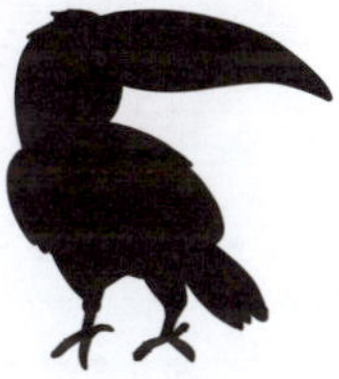

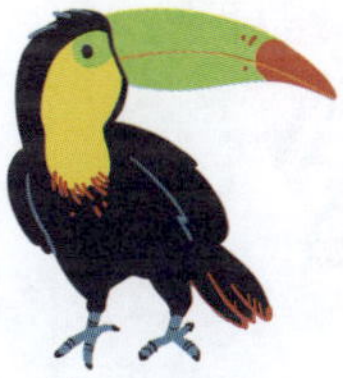
Toucan

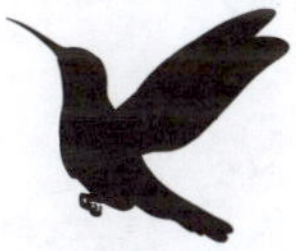

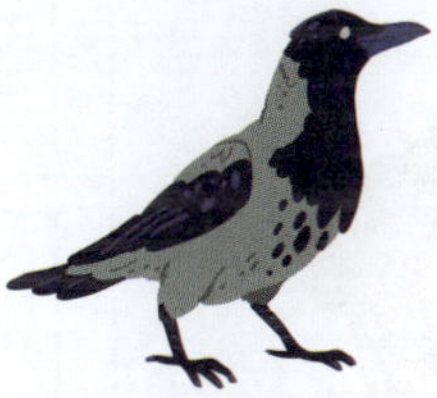
Crow

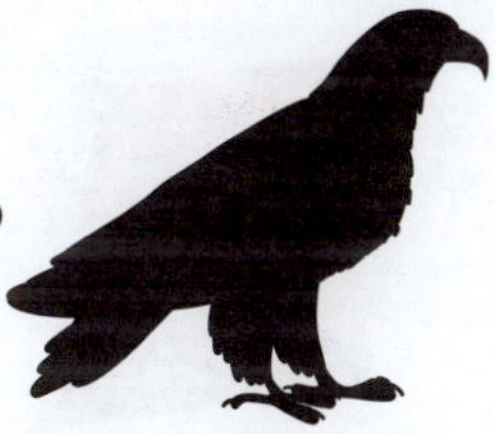

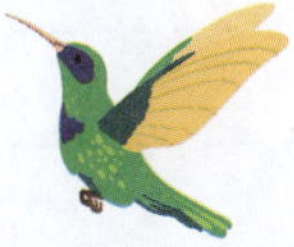
Hummingbird

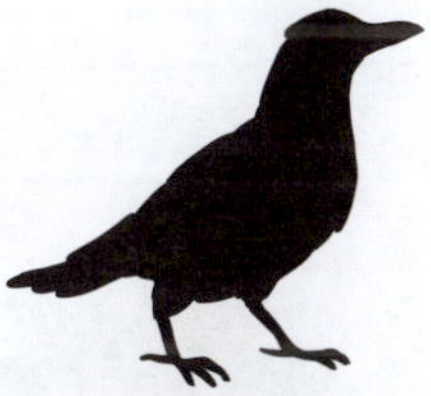

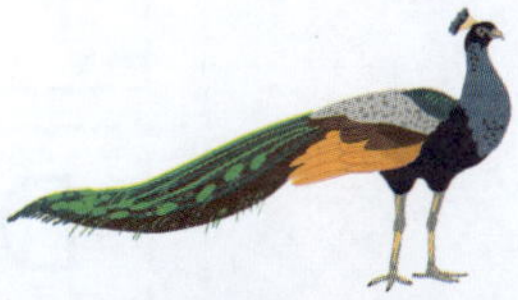
Peacock

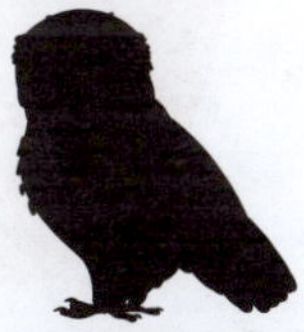

Colour the beginning letter of each picture

E
V
D

A
B
D

F
A
D

R
T
S

T
G
K

B
K
P

S
B
R

L
F
D

Match the vegetables with their slices

Beetroot

Bellpepper

Cucumber

Potato

Brinjal

Tomato

Cognitive Development

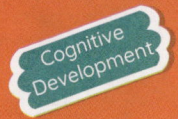

Circle the sandwich, which doesn't have a pair

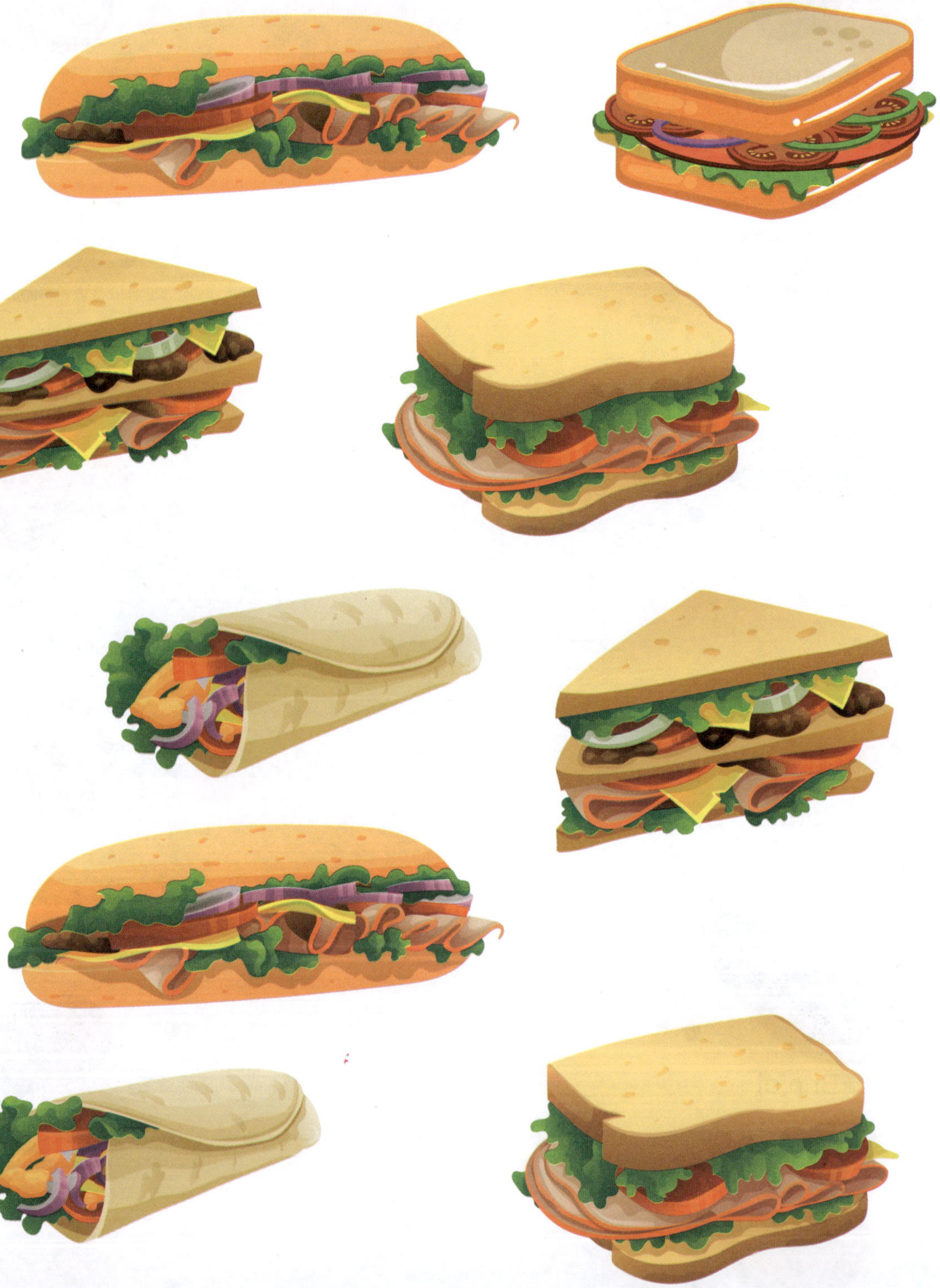

Match the means of transport to the community helper who uses them

Air Hostess

Police

Astronaut

Doctor

Firefighter

Literacy

Write the beginning letter of each picture

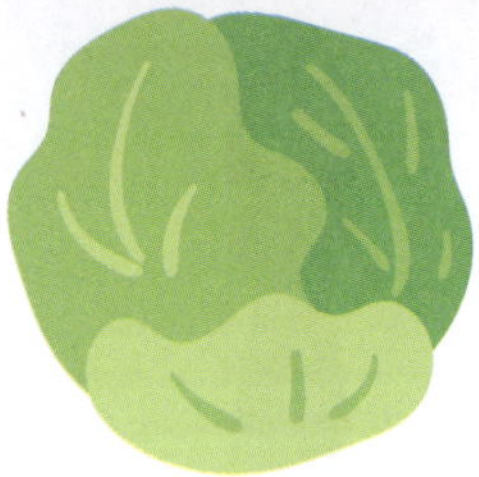

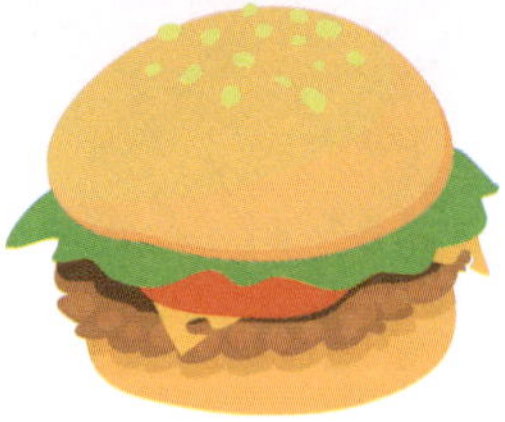

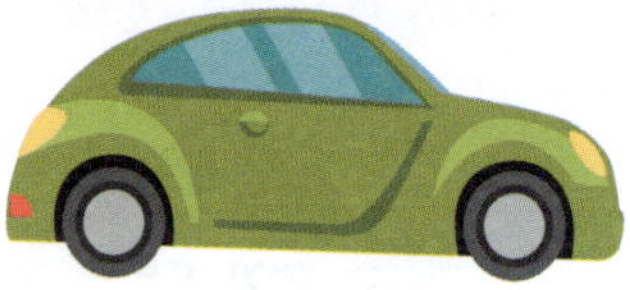

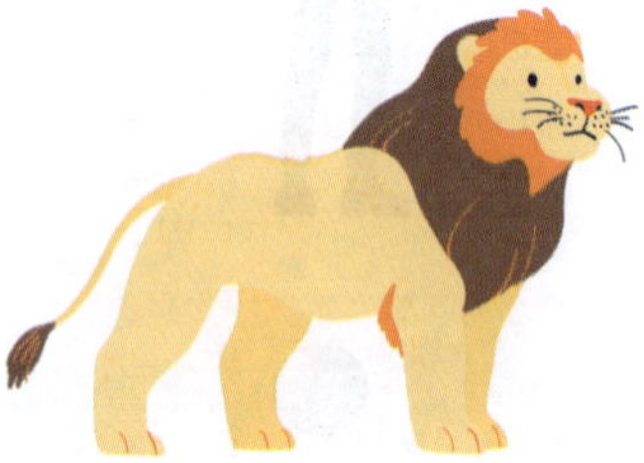

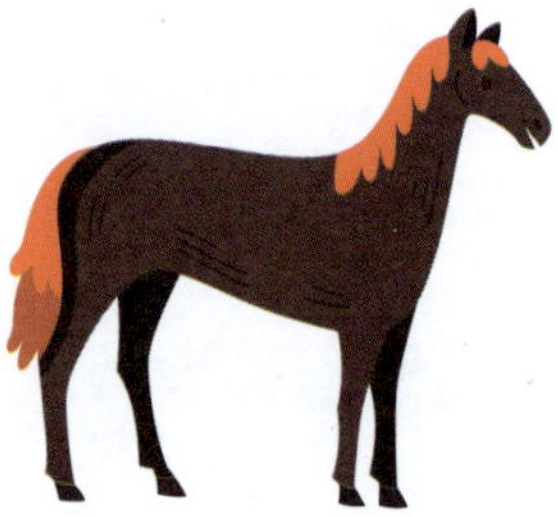

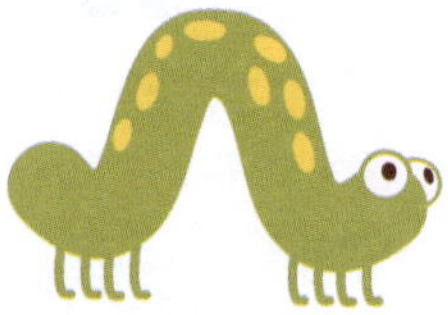

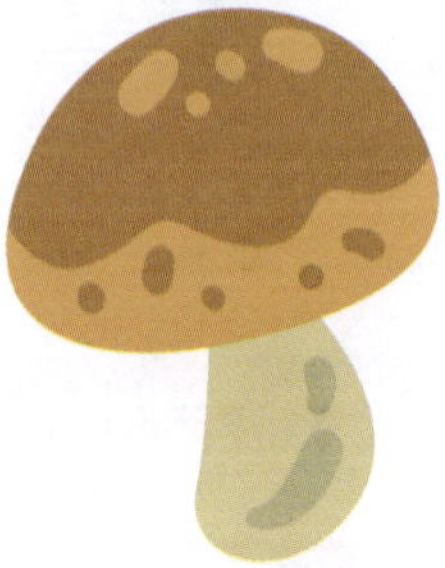

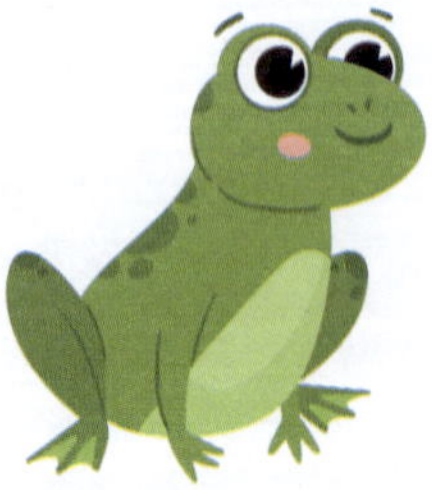

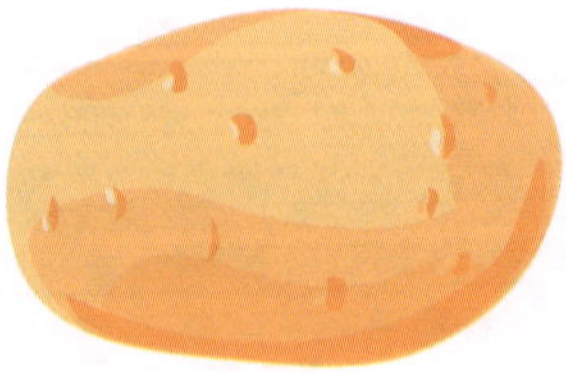

Find and circle the hidden objects

Numeracy

Count and write the number of animals

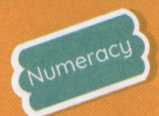

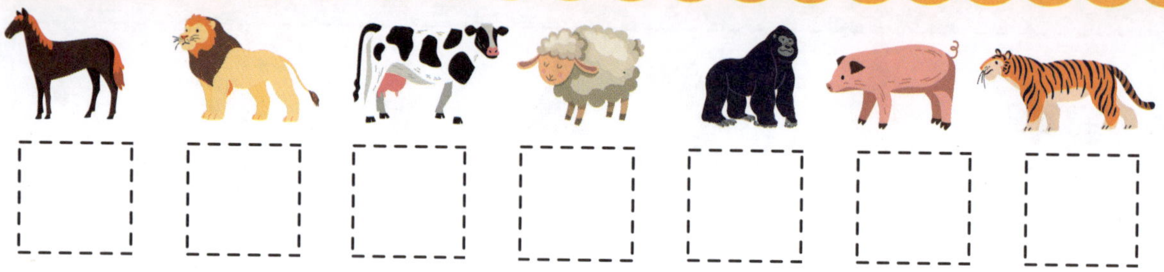

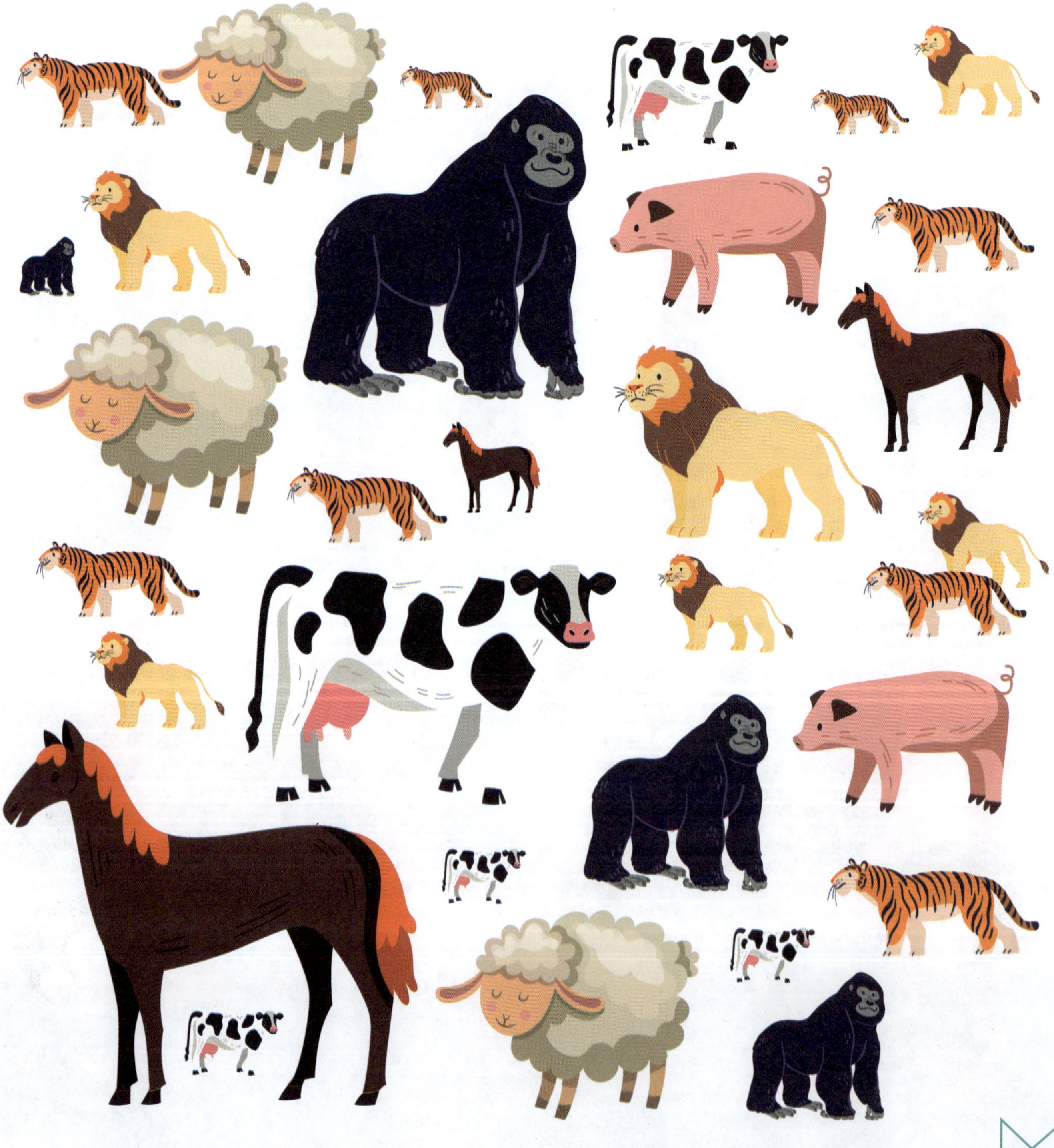

Spot and circle the differences

Spot and match the musical instruments

Cognitive Development

Follow the colour codes and colour the circles

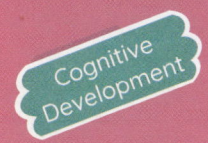

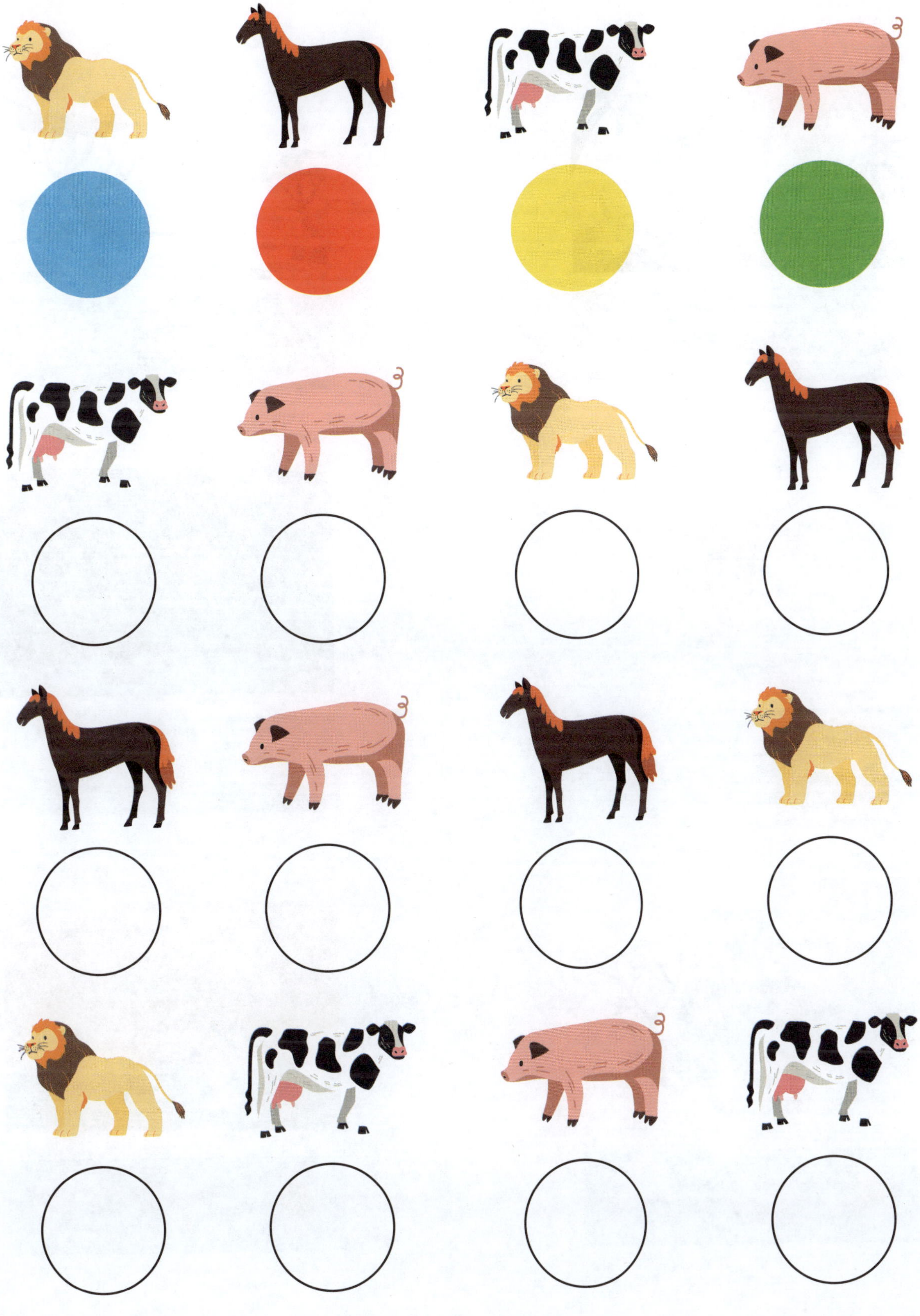

Look at the pictures and circle the season they represent

Write the beginning letter of the pictures given

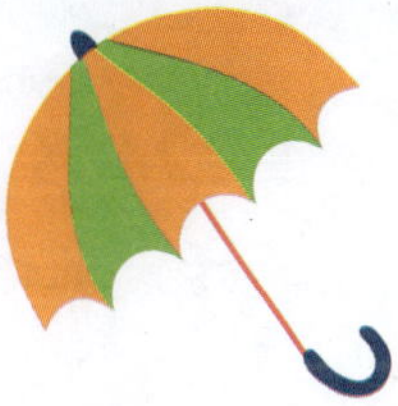

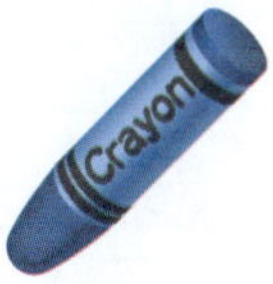

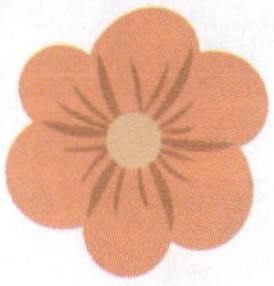

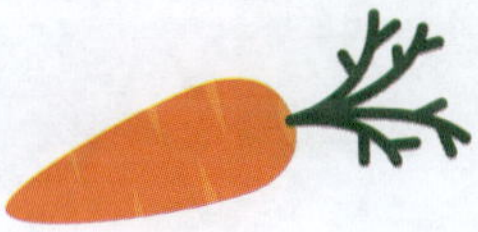

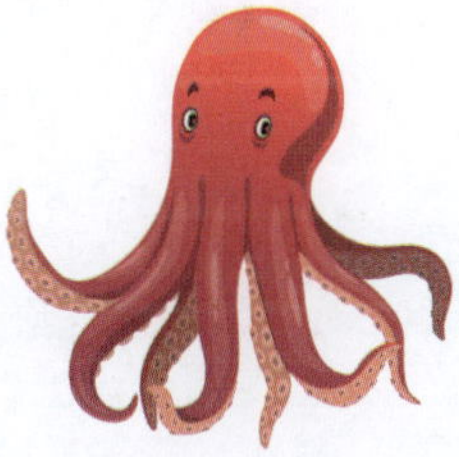

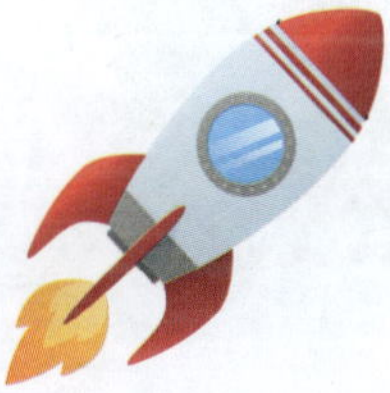

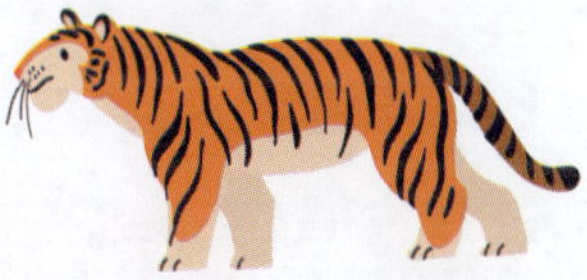

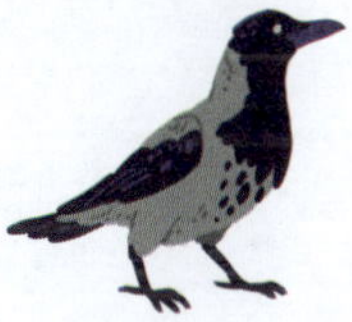

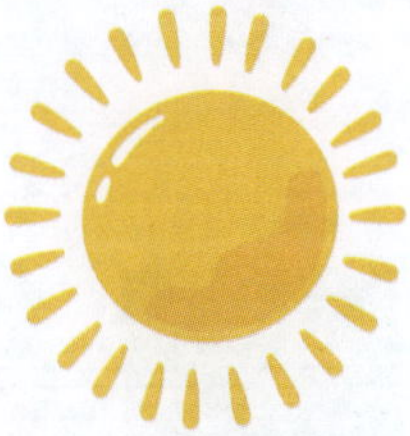

Match the same patterns

Match the uppercase letters with their lowercases

Cognitive Development

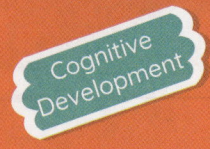

Match the same umbrellas

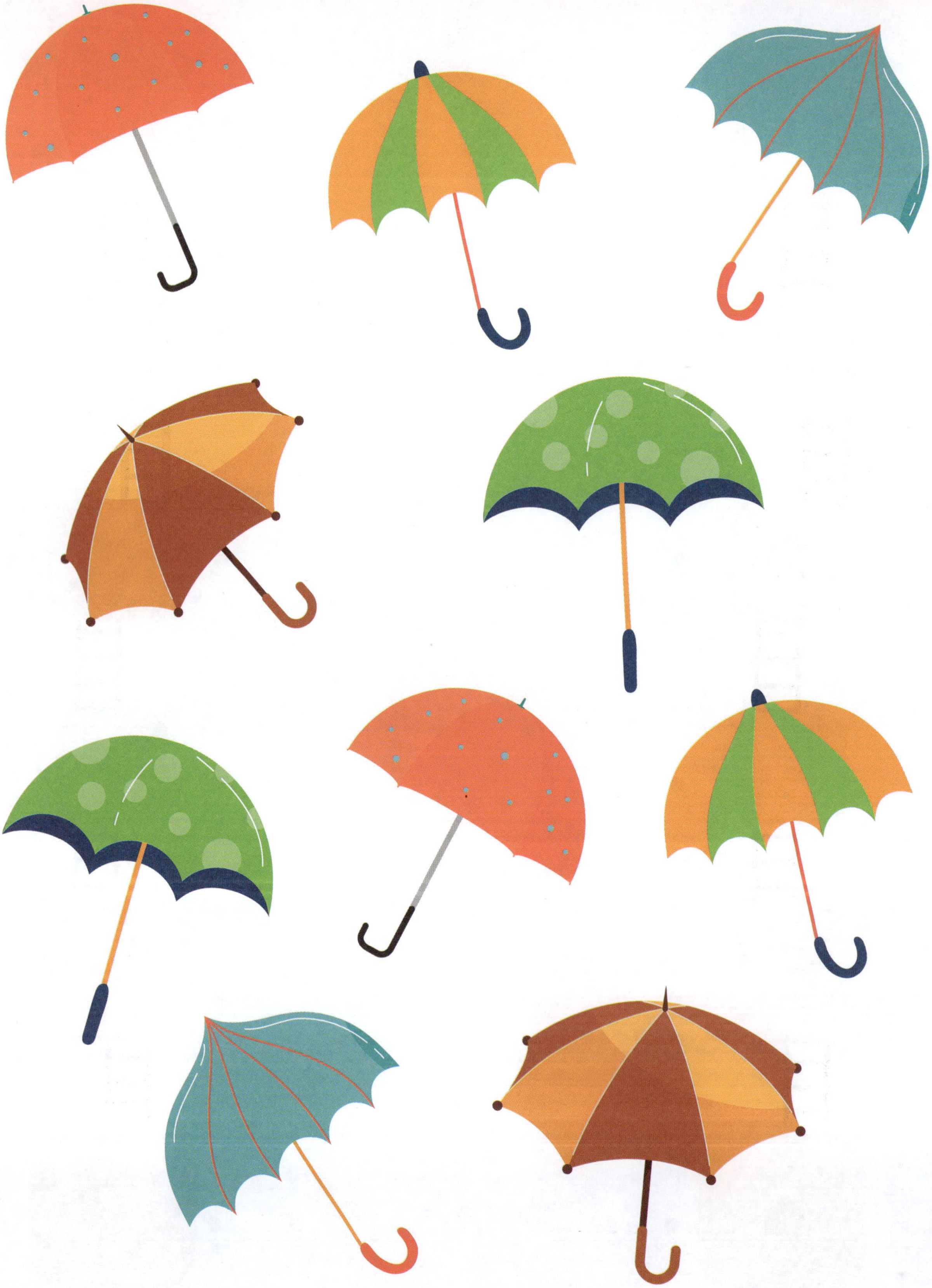

Literacy

Fill in the missing letters in the carrots

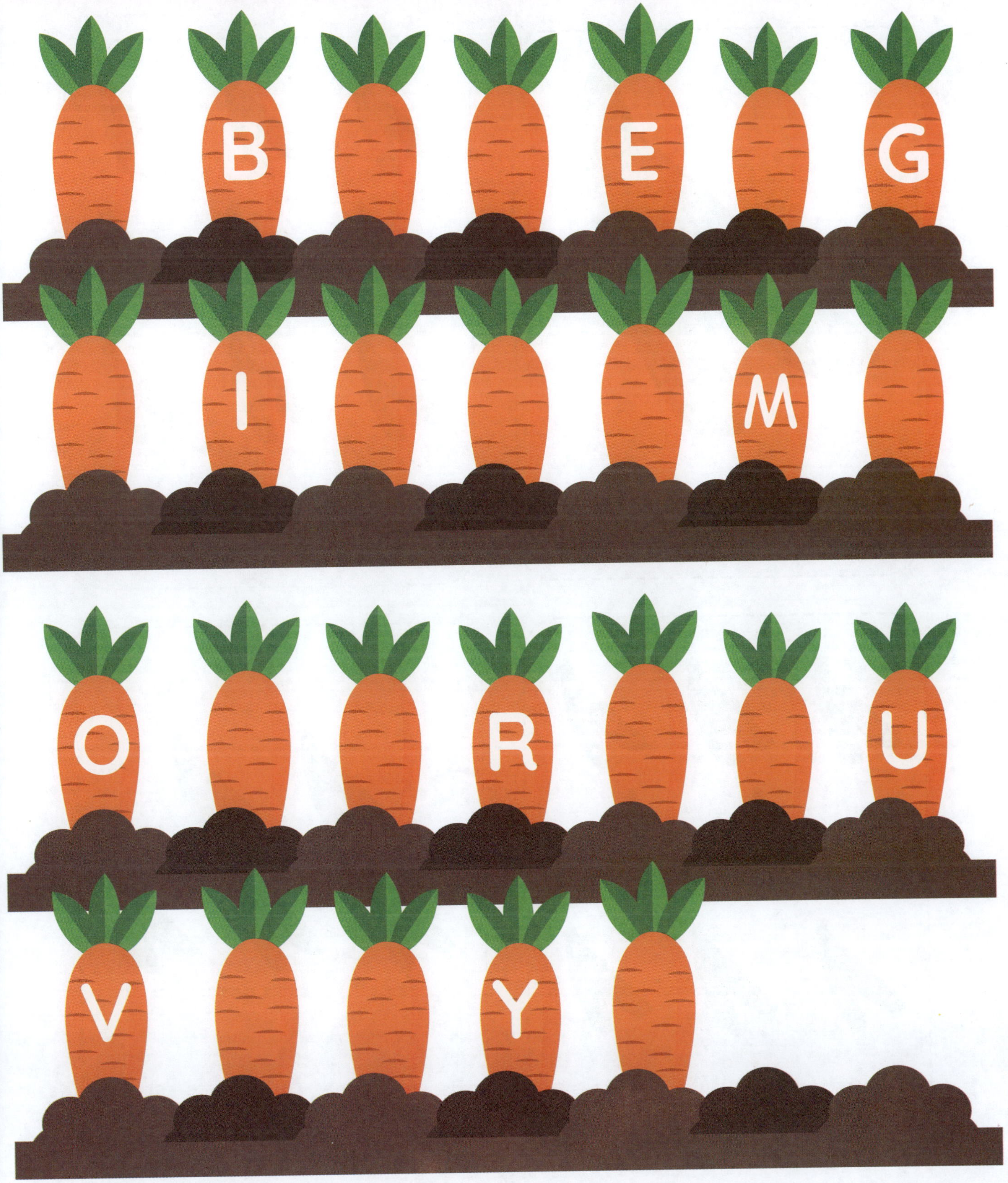

Count and circle the number of pods

2   1   5   3

9   8   6   1

7   9   8   6

2   4   3   5

Literacy

Write the beginning letter of each picture from the options given

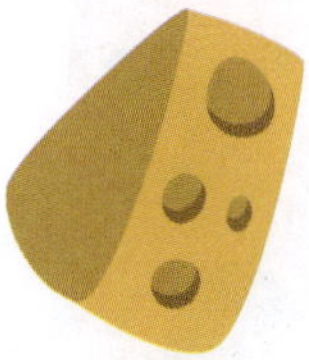

C E B

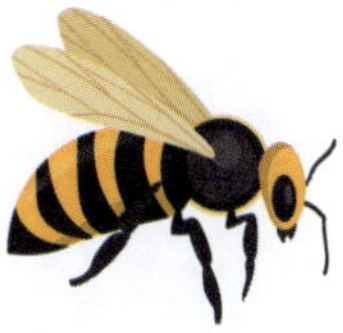

R V B

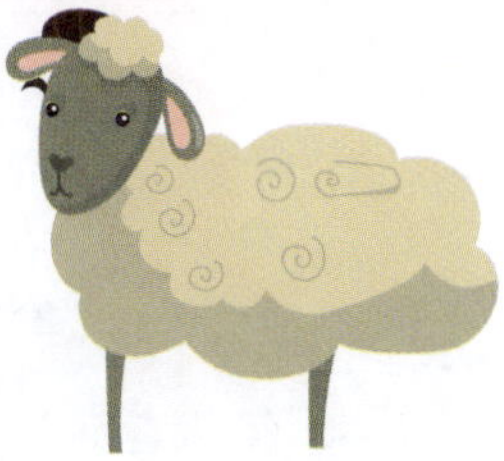

A S E

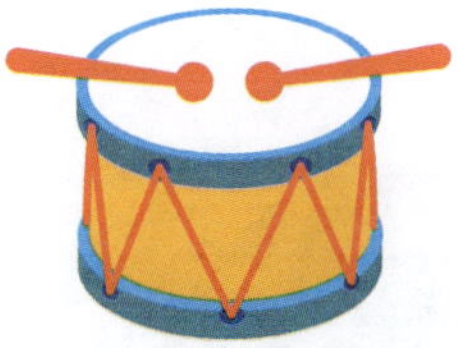

D Q O

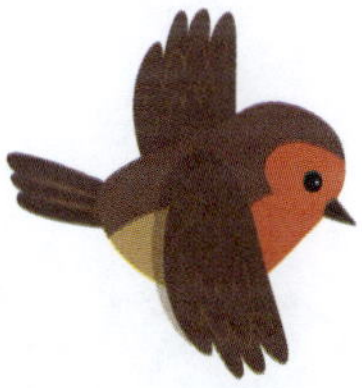

C B P

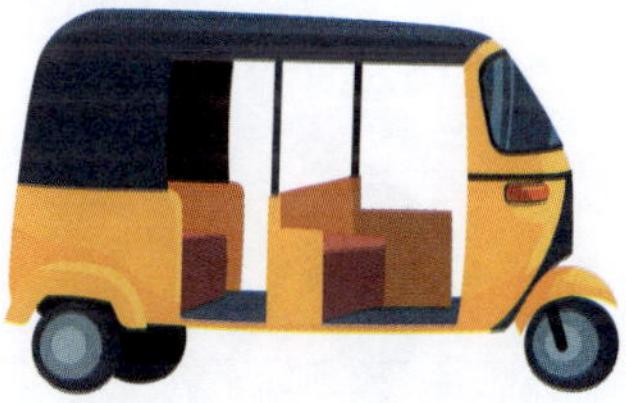

P R A

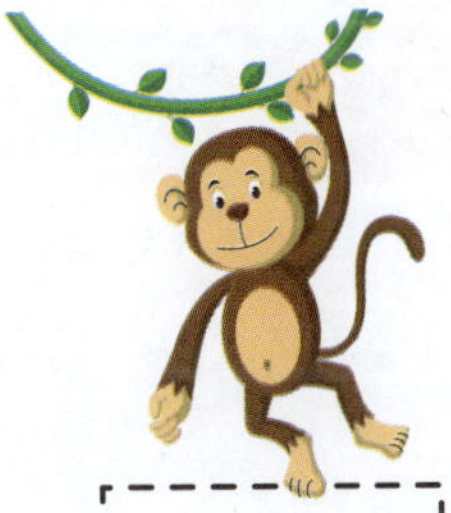

T M B

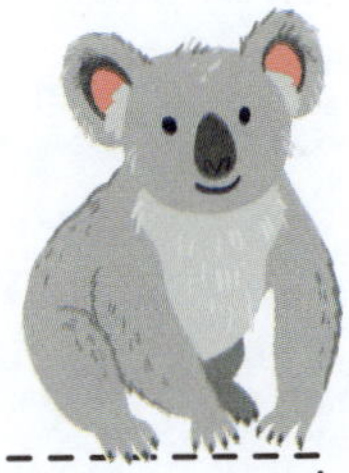

K Q B

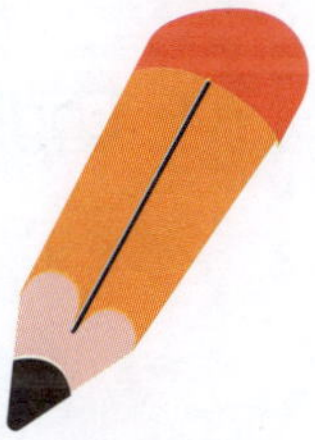

H L P

Match each animal to the correct pattern

Octopus

Worm

Sheep

Eagle

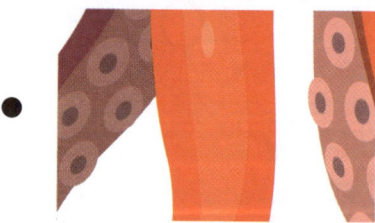

Beetle

A

V

B

R

E

W

Q

w

q

e

a

v

b

r

98

Find and circle the hidden letters

Choose the correct symbol to go with each image

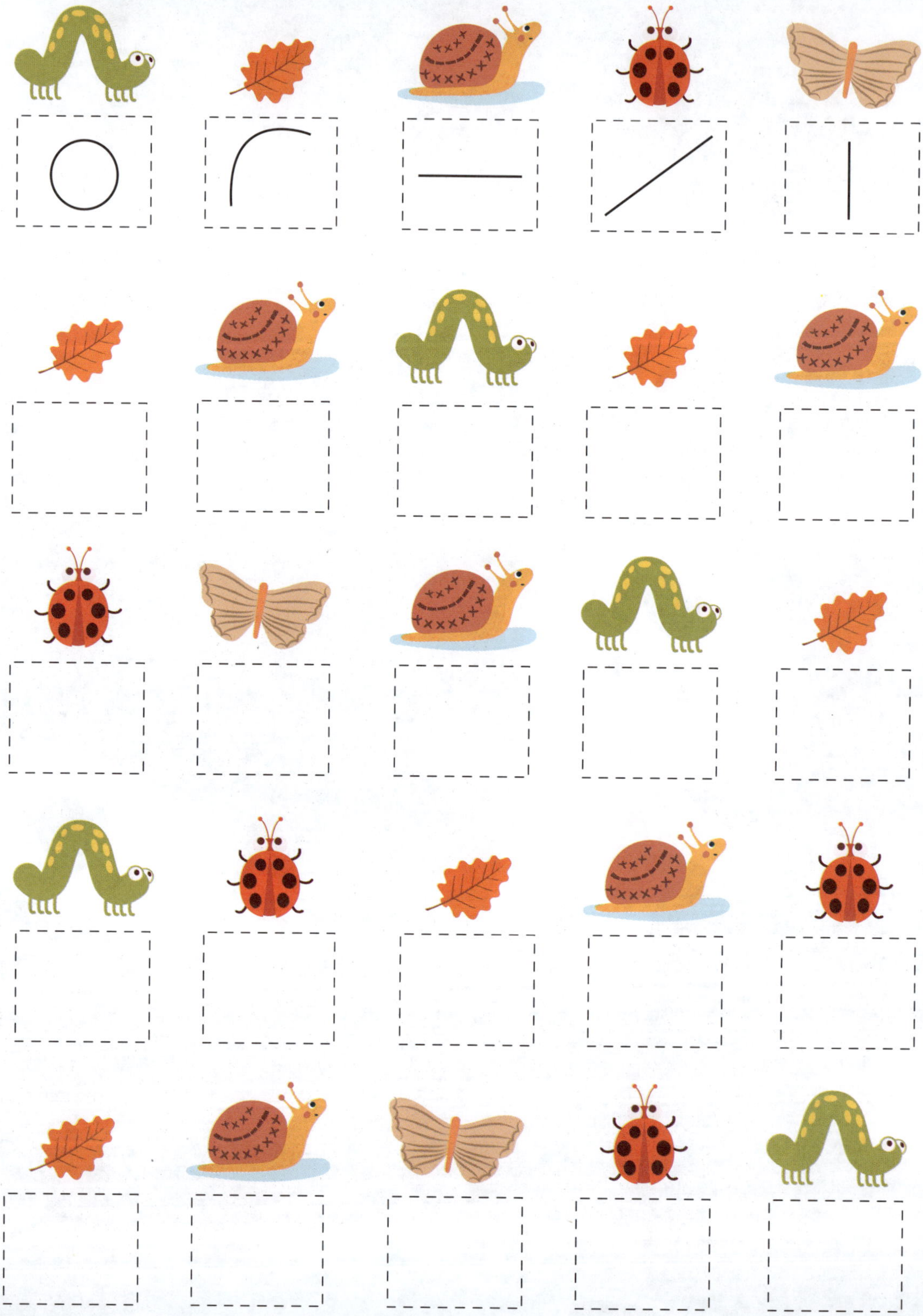

○ ⌐ — ╱ │

Read the instructions in each box and do as directed

Circle the one that flies

Circle the one that is a fruit.

Circle the one that gives light

Circle the one with stripes

Join the dots and make the same pattern

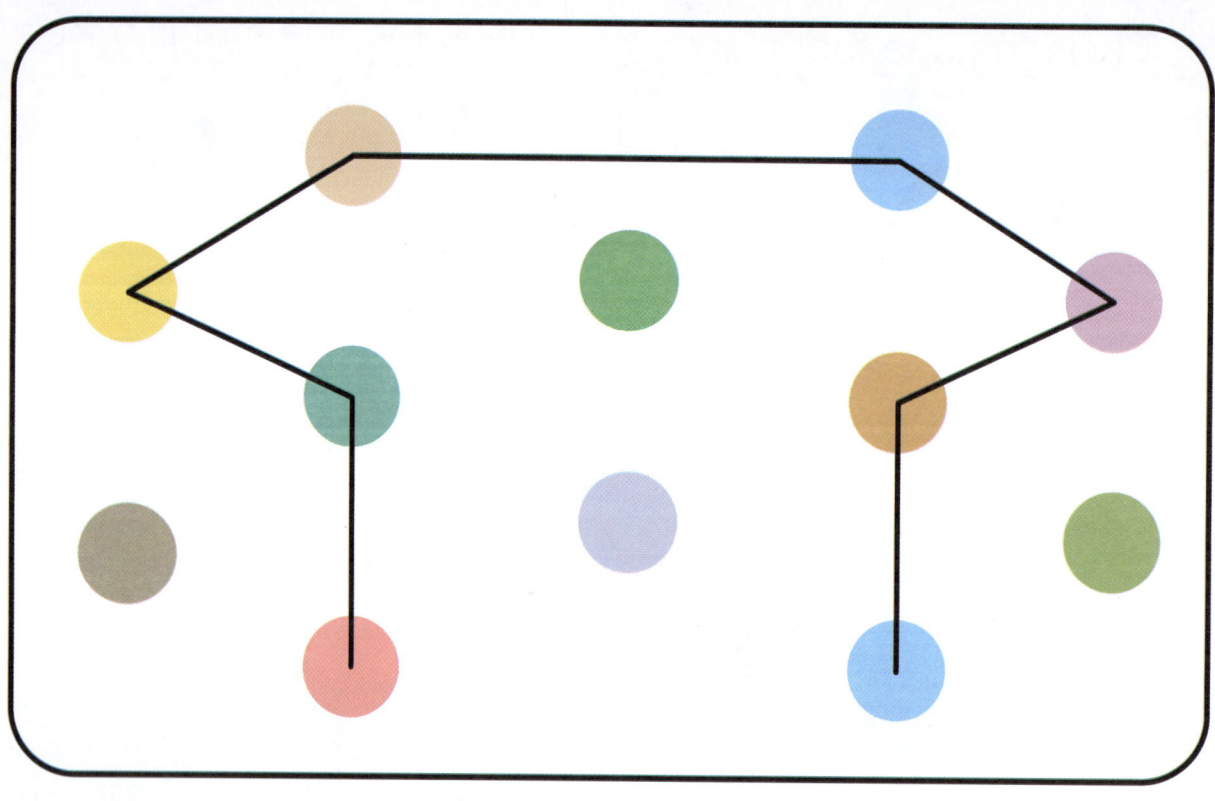

Match opposite pictures

Hot

Clean

Empty

Light on

Dirty

Full

Light Off

Cold

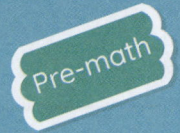

Let's colour the castle using the colour codes

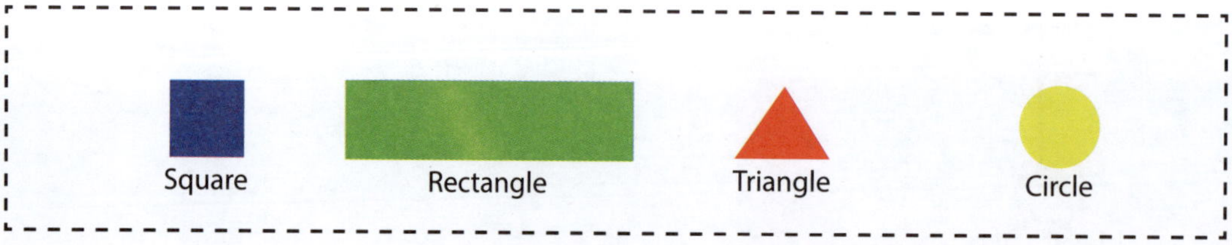

| Square | Rectangle | Triangle | Circle |

Find and circle the hidden numbers from 1 to 10

Literacy

Trace the uppercase letters and write the lowercase letters below

A B C D E F

G H I J K L

M N O P Q

R S T U V

W X Y Z

Numeracy

Use the given colour codes and colour the picture

1 2 3 4 5

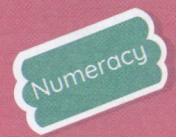

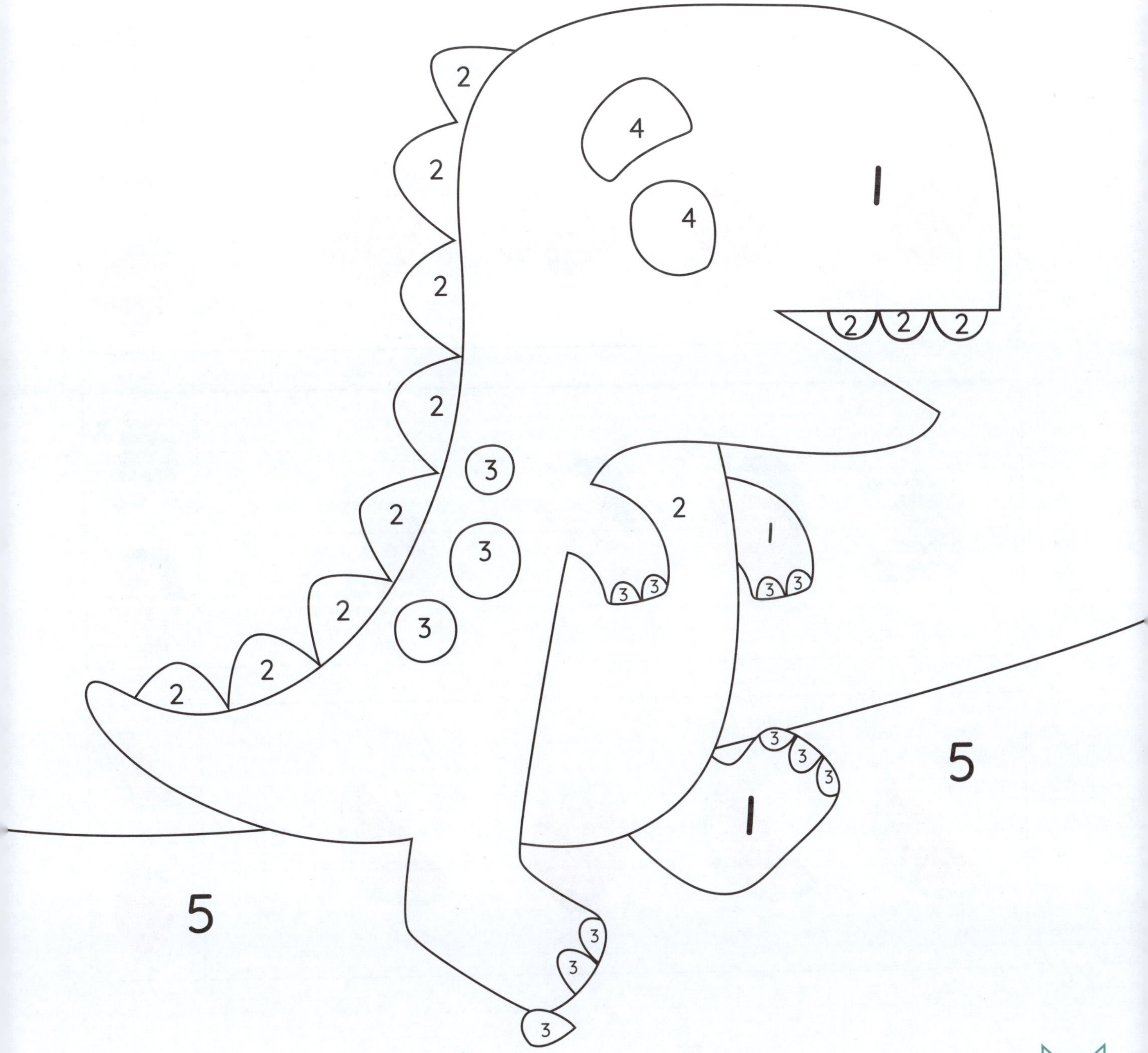

Circle the correct answer and complete the pattern

Join the dots and colour the picture

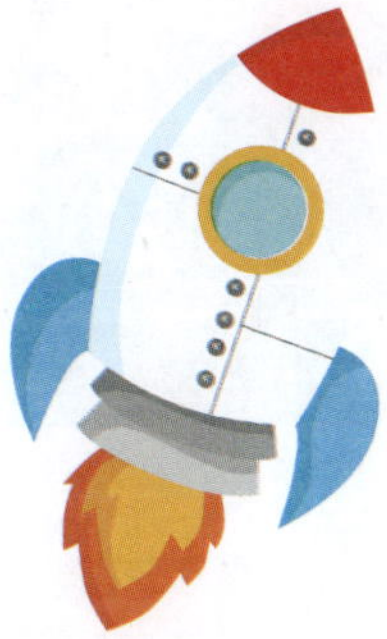

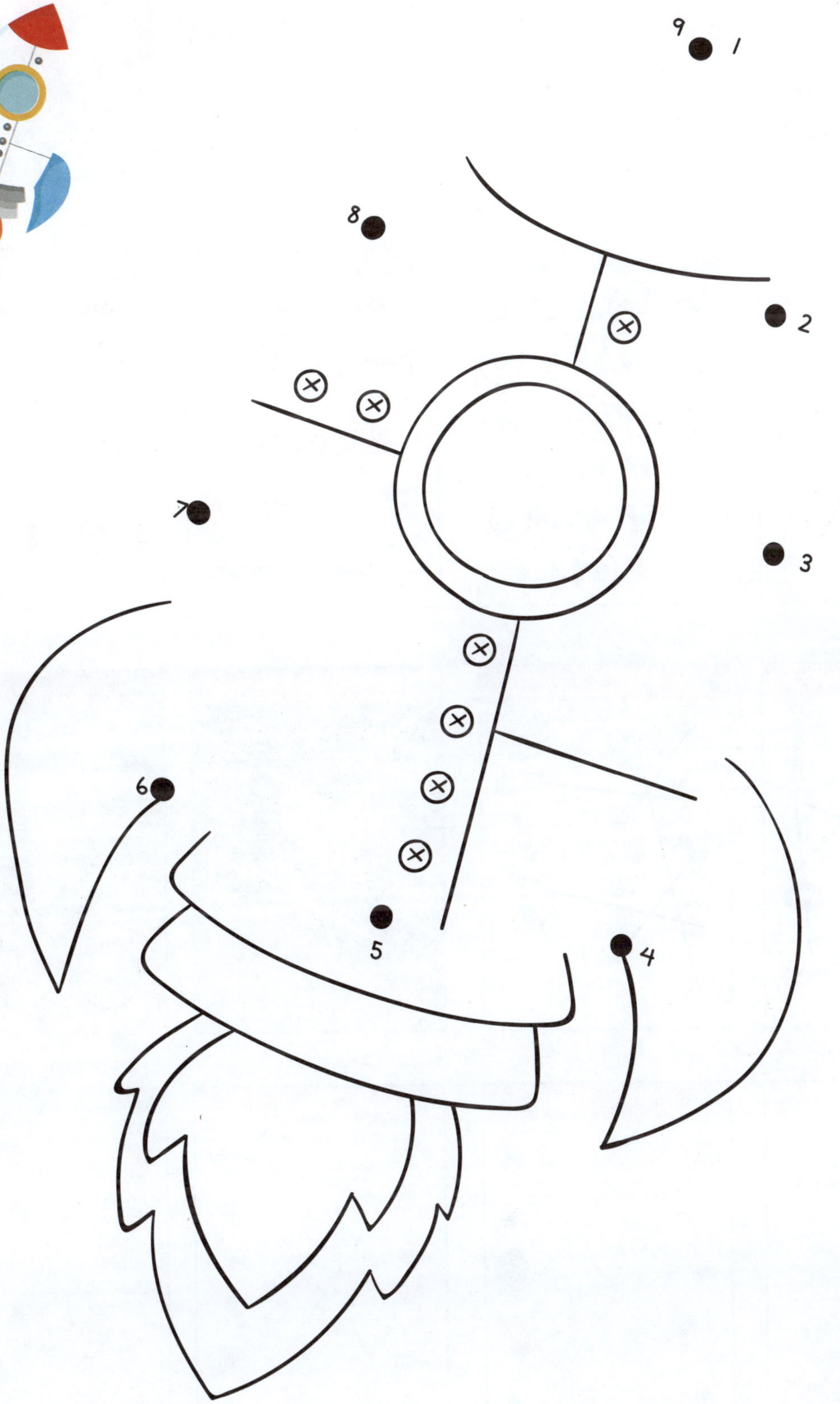

9 ● ／ 1

8 ●

⊗

● 2

⊗   ⊗

7 ●

● 3

⊗

⊗

⊗

6 ●

⊗

5 ●

● 4

Answer sheet

Pg no. 11

Pg no. 14

Pg no. 15

Pg no. 16

Pg no. 18

Pg no. 20

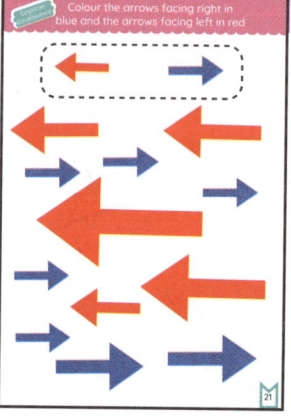

Pg no. 21

Pg no. 22

Pg no. 23

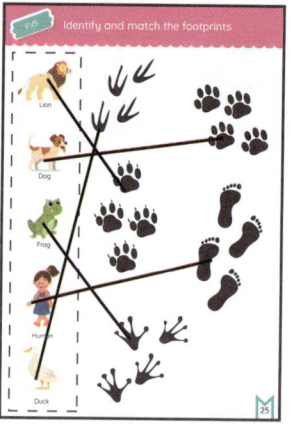

Pg no. 25

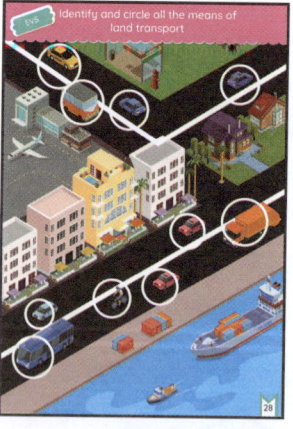

Pg no. 28

Pg no. 29

Pg no. 30

Pg no. 33

Pg no. 35

Pg no. 36

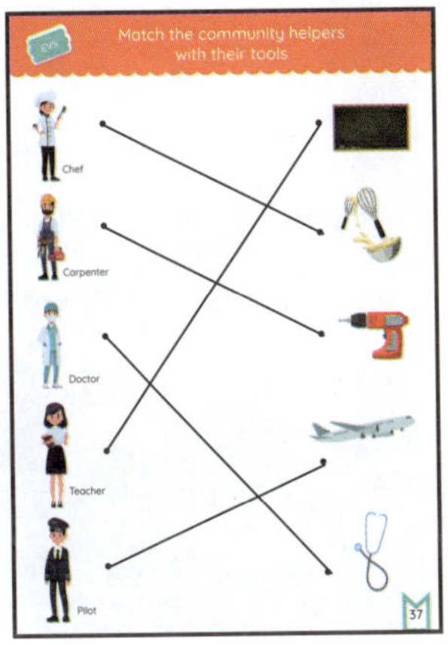

Match the community helpers with their tools

Chef
Carpenter
Doctor
Teacher
Pilot

Pg no. 37

Observe the shape on the side and encircle the identical shape

Pg no. 38

Fill in the missing numbers on the caterpillars

1 2 3 4 5
11 12 13 14 15
5 6 7 8 9
15 16 17 18 19
16 17 18 19 20

Pg no. 39

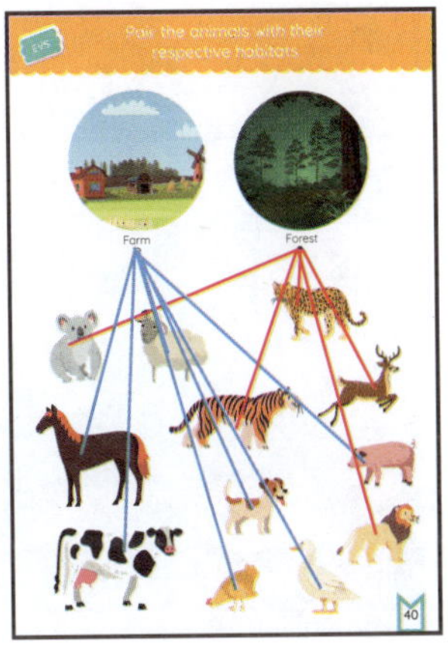

Pair the animals with their respective habitats

Farm   Forest

Pg no. 40

Help the dog reach the kennel by by completing the missing letters

A B C D E F G H
R Q P O N M L K J I
S T U V W X Y Z a b c d
m l k j i h g f e
n o p q r s t u v w x y z

Pg no. 41

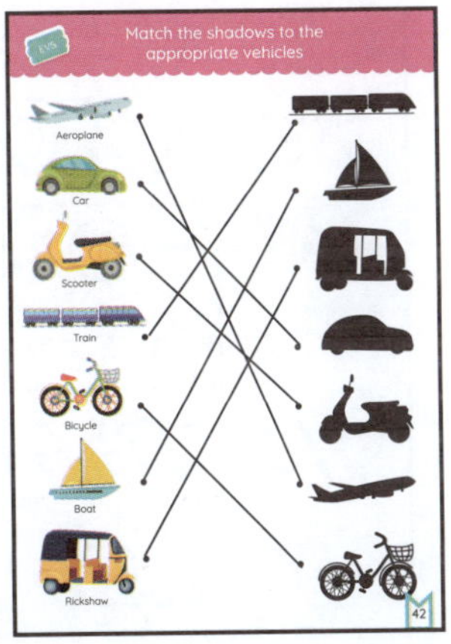

Match the shadows to the appropriate vehicles

Aeroplane
Car
Scooter
Train
Bicycle
Boat
Rickshaw

Pg no. 42

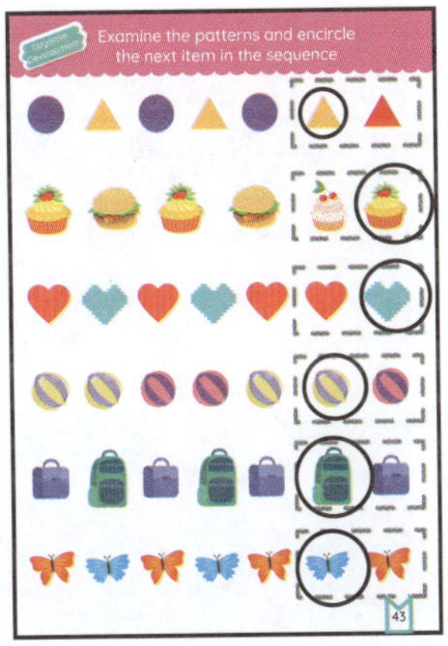

Examine the patterns and encircle the next item in the sequence

Pg no. 43

Match the young animals to their parents

Pg no. 46

Match the pictures that go together

Pg no. 48

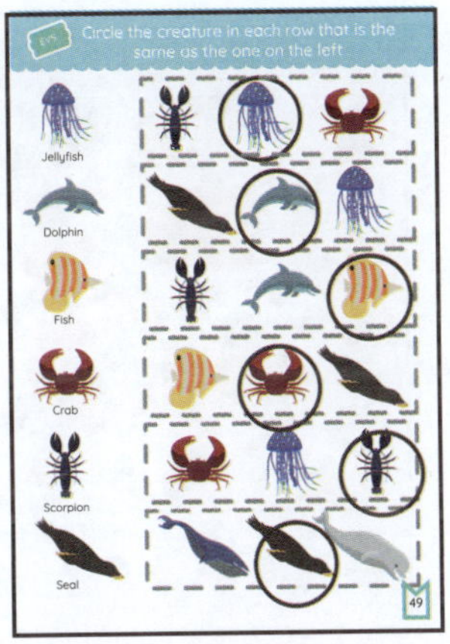

Circle the creature in each row that is the same as the one on the left

Jellyfish
Dolphin
Fish
Crab
Scorpion
Seal

Pg no. 49

Observe the objects and match them to their correct shape

Pg no. 50

Count and write the number of animals and birds

5   4   7   2   7

Pg no. 52

Identify and circle all the birds

Pg no. 53

Match each mode of transport to its corresponding vehicle

Truck
Boat
Car
Helicopter
Bus
Aeroplane
Van
Ship

Pg no. 54

Match the animals to their shadows

Pg no. 57

Count and circle the groups with less objects

Pg no. 58

Pg no. 59

Pg no. 61

Pg no. 62

Pg no. 63

Pg no. 64

Pg no. 65

Pg no. 66

Pg no. 67

Pg no. 68

Pg no. 69

Pg no. 70

Pg no. 71

Pg no. 72

Pg no. 73

Pg no. 74

Pg no. 75

Pg no. 76

Pg no. 77

Pg no. 78

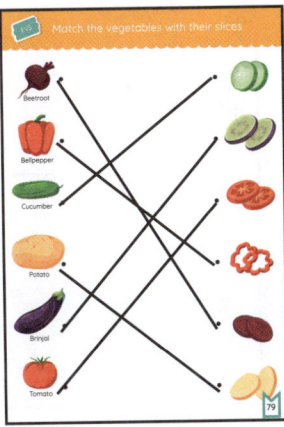

Pg no. 79

Pg no. 80

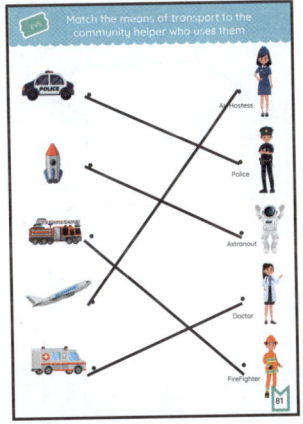

Pg no. 81

Pg no. 82

Pg no. 83

Pg no. 84

Pg no. 85

Pg no. 86

Pg no. 87

Pg no. 88

Pg no. 89

Pg no. 90

Pg no. 94

Pg no. 95

Pg no. 96

Pg no. 98

Pg no. 99

Pg no. 100

Pg no. 101

Pg no. 102

Pg no. 103

Pg no. 105

Pg no. 106

Pg no. 108

Pg no. 109

CHAMPAK

CERTIFICATE
of Completion

THIS CERTIFICATE IS PROUDLY PRESENTED TO

for sucessful completion of book K activities in

little fingers **Big Brains**

Date

Signature